Introduction

For many people, the chance to visit Egypt is a lifetime event. In my role as Minister of Tourism, it is my pleasure to make sure that these visitors' expectations for a rewarding tour of Egypt are not only met but exceeded. This new book, *In the Eye of Horus*, has met and exceeded all my expectations of presenting a spectacular and astonishing new view of Egypt.

Many of us are aware of the splendor of Egypt's pharaonic monuments and natural beauties. We tour the monuments with educated guides, enduring sun and heat to gain insight on the wealth of Egypt's past. Or perhaps we make adventurous treks to enjoy the bounty and variety of Egypt's landscapes. But despite all our best efforts, it is often difficult to put these monuments and natural environments into a new and exciting perspective that gives us a true sense of their context in the landscape of the country. This book, with its stunning aerial views and satellite photographs proceeds to do just that.

Through the camera lens of internationally renowned landscape photographer Marcello Bertinetti, the reader is taken on a journey over Egypt from a bird's-eye point of view. From this aerial vantage point, the complicated but beautiful logic of the monuments on the Giza plateau becomes suddenly clear, and one can see the relationships between the pyramids, their valley temples, their satellite pyramids, and the silent Sphinx, as well as the growing city of Cairo. And the austere majesty of the pyramids presents a striking contrast with images of bustling Cairo, one of the greatest cities of the world.

Luxor, Aswan, and Nubia also come alive on these pages. In addition to soaring views of the colossal temples of Abu Simbel and the grandeur of Queen Hatshepsut's temple of Deir al-Bahari, we are able to look surprisingly closely at the rhythms of everyday life in the southern countryside. We see the patchwork quilt of fields being cultivated and harvested as well as the patterns of homes and human traffic in the villages. All the while, the photographs make us aware of the fragile boundaries between the desert and the cultivated areas so necessary to Egyptian life.

The sections of the book depicting the Sinai Peninsula, the Red Sea coasts, and the shoreline of Egypt's northern coast illustrate different boundaries and relationships. The jewel-tone blues and greens of the sea and coral reefs around the Ras Muhammad National Park at the southernmost point of Sinai reflect a corner of paradise, while the ravishing turquoise waters of Egypt's Mediterranean coast invite us to dive right in. And the remarkable symbiosis of Egypt's land and water is further demonstrated by the engineering marvels of the Suez Canal, which are depicted with wonderful clarity and detail.

Finally, the series of images from a NASA satellite complete the tour by putting Egypt firmly in her position on the globe. From this distance one can clearly recognize the lotus flower formed by the path of the Nile as it winds from Upper Egypt then blossoms in the Delta. From Alexandria to Nubia, from the desert oases to the burgeoning cities, *In the Eye of Horus* truly captures the balance between man and nature, desert and green, past and present in these extraordinary photographs. I encourage everyone with an interest in Egypt to pause and join me on this incredible new tour of our beautiful country.

H.E. Dr Mamdouh El-Beltagui
The Egyptian Minister of Tourism

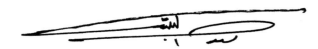

8 An obelisk of Ramesses II in front of the pylon in the Temple of Luxor. Originally the pylon was flanked by another obelisk, which now stands in the Place de la Concorde in Paris.

10-11 A lake of mineral-rich water stands out from the Western Desert near Lake Qarun in Fayoum oasis

12-13 A caravan of camels files past the ruins of the temple on Wadi al-Sebua.

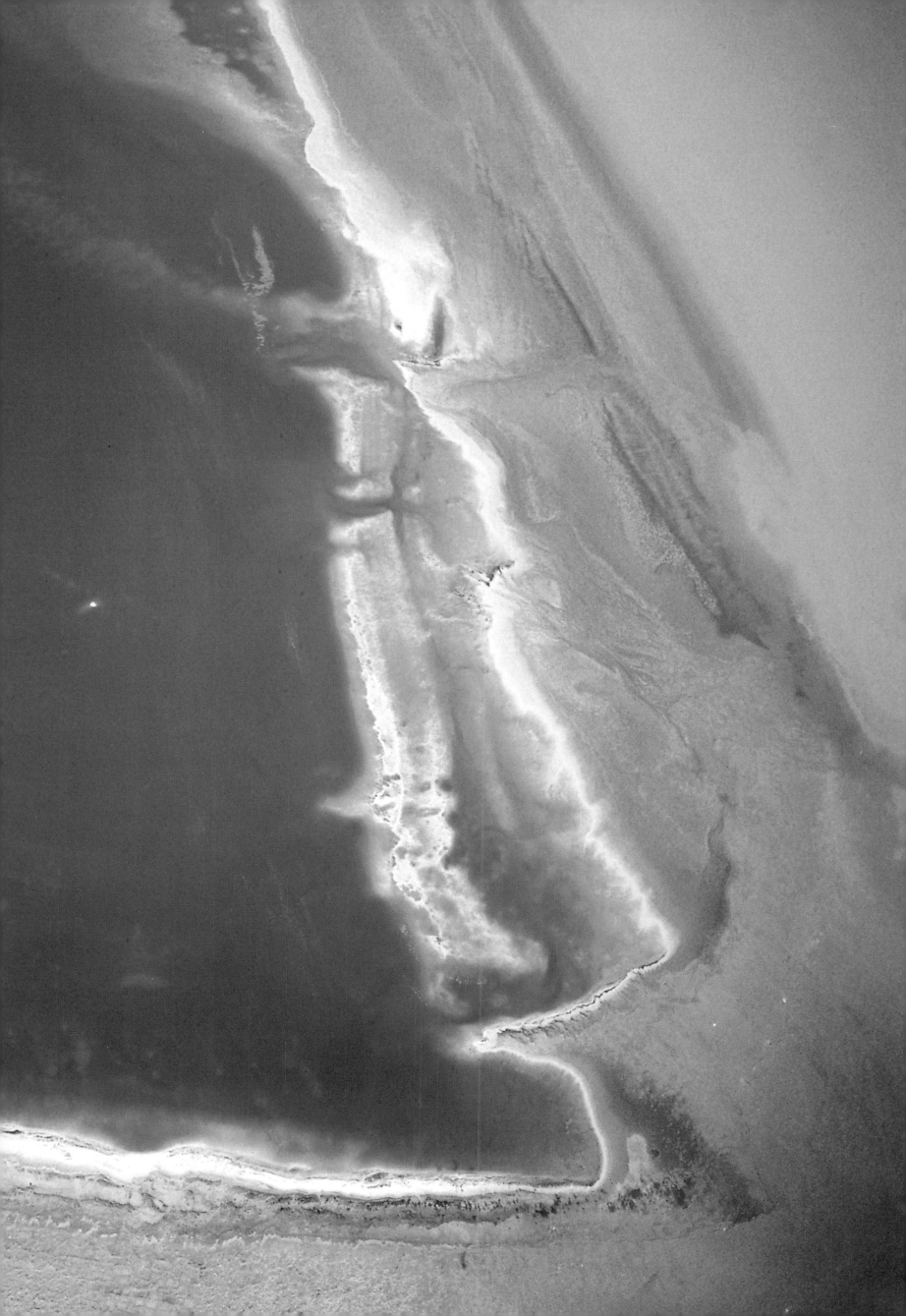

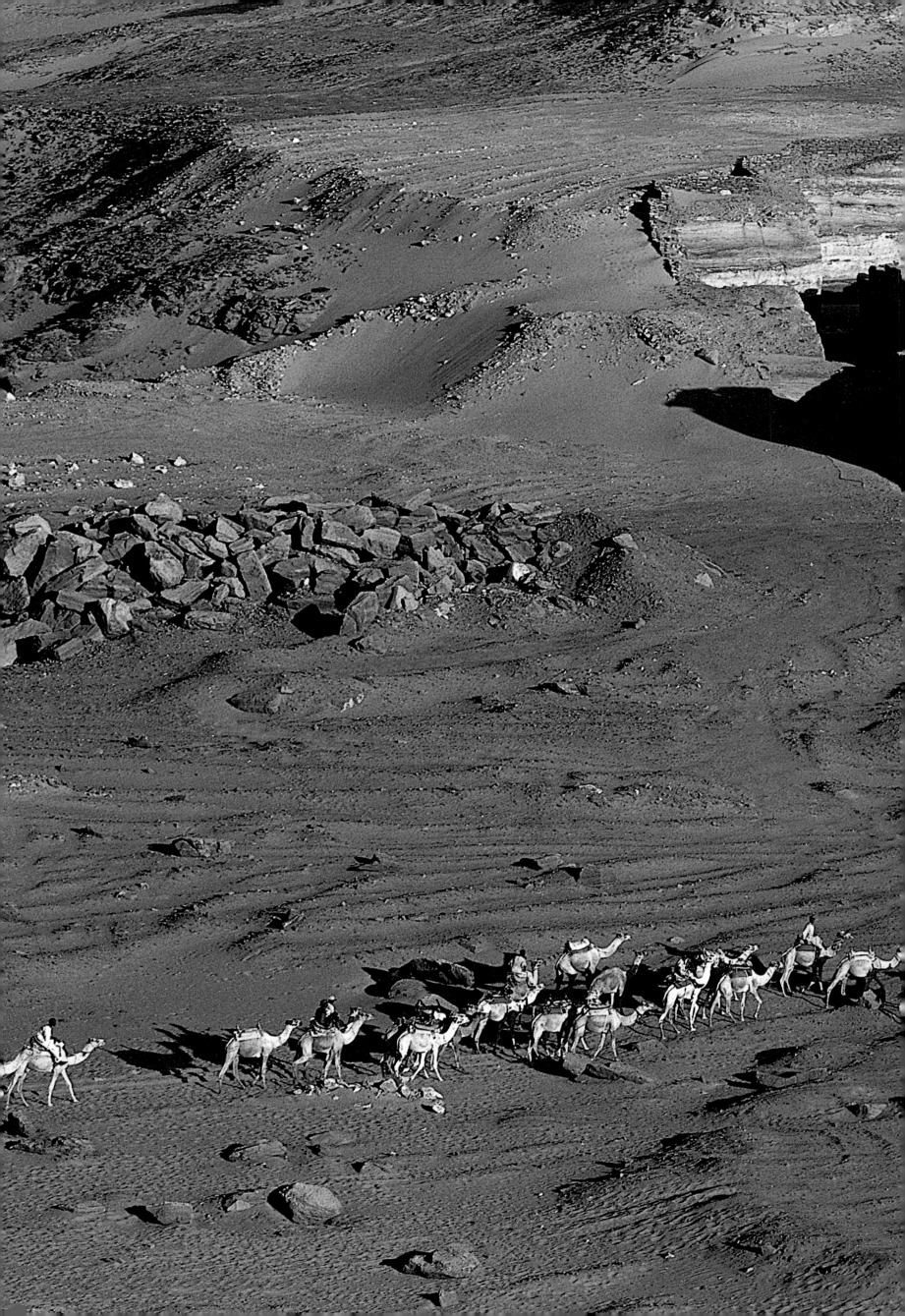

A Photographer's Flight over Egypt

by Marcello Bertinetti

At times I close my eyes and it seems I am still there, trussed with steel wires, hanging out the side of a doorless helicopter at dawn one magical morning.

I was flying over Upper Egypt, on the shores of Lake Nasser, far from anywhere else, lost among the blue and ocher of the water and desert. The noise was unbelievable, but I didn't hear it because I was in a trance. I was concentrating on the image, which from the air is often impersonal and cold, because I wanted these pictures to reflect me, my taste, my personality, and my human warmth.

Suddenly I noticed three ancient Egyptian temples standing on a sandy promontory. They seemed abandoned. I recognized them despite our rapid approach: Wadi al-Sebua, Dakka, and Maharraqa. They were wonderful.

By 6:30 the light had turned warmer. I checked the cameras and gave instructions to the pilot. I was ready to shoot when all of a sudden, a group of camels guided by a Bedouin came out of nowhere. We were about 300 meters from the temple and, in the excitement of the moment, I shouted at the pilot to change direction and head for the caravan. Behind me, my friend Mark Linz and our guide Gamal Shafik had got to their feet. Mark kept saying, "It's fantastic! It's fantastic!"

I began to get nervous. I clutched the camera and got ready to shoot, but the helicopter was not positioned how I wanted it to be and I couldn't get the shot. It seemed a sort of sacrilege. We made another circle . . . another failure . . . then two more. I was furious and started to shout at the pilot while Gamal tried to translate. The air was hitting me full in the face as I leaned almost completely out of the helicopter. Suddenly I was looking at a scene that made me gasp: the camels were slowly making their way past the temple of Wadi al-Sebua and the helicopter had moved to a perfect angle . . . the trajectories complemented one another perfectly and caught them right in front of the temple.

I had four to five seconds to prepare for the shot. I checked how many frames I had available and chose the lens, a Nikon 135 mm f2.0; I set the speed at one-thousandth of a second and the f-stop at four. I was ready and focused. I shot, shot again, and yet again. I was cold, impassive, not allowing any emotion in that might have spoiled the shot. I had about three seconds available and I took at least a dozen pictures.

Suddenly the helicopter was far away, the camels had passed the temple and the first tourists were arriving by boat from their cruise ship. Almost as if by magic, the light was changing too. I checked the camera, everything was okay. I rewound the film and put it in my pocket. It was mine.

How can I describe the experiences I had flying over Egypt without getting emotional and feeling the excitement rise in me at my good fortune? What I had seen was exceptional, and the pictures can only vaguely convey my feelings. But inside me there is a well of knowledge that contains each one of the 15,000 shots that I took. I only have to close my eyes and reach in.

My trip through the skies over Egypt began in Cairo on a gloomy September morning. I was heading south toward Hurghada and the Red Sea. We left the outskirts of the huge, chaotic city and suddenly we were in the desert. My first shots were of the beautiful and isolated Coptic monasteries of St. Paul and St. Antony, close to the coast of the Red Sea. Then we went on to Ras al-Bahr where the loveliest coral sea in the world lay beneath my feet in all its splendor. Glorious reefs alternated with crystaline lagoons, and the various shades of green and blue mingled as though in a kaleidoscope.

Then we were over the Gubal Strait, north of Hurghada, where there is a myriad of tiny islands and coral reefs. I saw several dive boats, a lighthouse far out among the reefs, strips of land in the middle of the sea and waves breaking violently against them. A few minutes later we landed at Hurghada, and after lunch took off again for Sharm al-Sheikh and Sinai.

Once across the Gubal Strait, with the island of Shadwan behind us, we approached Ras Muhammad promontory on the southern tip of Sinai. Memories flooded my mind when I saw that spur of rock:
I remembered when I spent months alone with my friends Carlo, Gianni, and Sergio on those superb beaches and in those unexplored seas. I was twenty; how much time has passed and how many things have happened since then!

The helicopter did not give me time to reflect: Ras

15 The white sands and turquoise water of the Red Sea make the coral reefs near Ras Gharib, north of Hurghada, some of the loveliest in Egypt.

Muhammad was already just a few minutes away. It stuck out into the blue of the Red Sea like a giant finger. It was wonderful, like living through a dream. Thank you, Ras Muhammad, you don't know how important you have been to me.

I gave the pilot instructions to fly higher so I could get a shot that would include everything. Unfortunately the day was muggy and I was unable to see the splendid rocky mountains of Sinai in the background. We came down and passed across the tip of the promontory that is a favorite haunt of divers and a place of unmatched natural beauty. Here the coral barrier drops vertically from the surface to a depth of 600 meters. The mixture of the currents of the gulfs of Aqaba and Suez gives rise to an incredible variety of underwater life. From the helicopter I could not see the colors of the gorgonia, alcyonaria, the coral, or the fish that I knew so well, but in my mind I was in the silence of the deep among those marvels of nature—seemingly near but so far away. We headed for Sharm al-Sheikh and Naama Bay, which is now a tourist area of major importance: the white, winding buildings of the hotels were the last sight of the day.

The next day we headed north once more toward the reefs of the Tiran Strait: Gordon, Thomas, Woodhouse, and Jackson, set like stones in the blue sea. They seem to reach the surface from unfathomable depths to protect the entrance to the Gulf of Aqaba. We headed for Tiran Island, a mountain of yellow desert with magnificent reefs and lagoons the color of emerald placed in the middle of the sea. I made out a wreck, the Maria Schroeder, seemingly asleep on the reef on the coast at the edge of Naba National Park. Then we flew over Dahab at speed and into Sinai.

The landscape changed completely. I still had the blues and greens of the sea in my eyes, when suddenly I was flying over dried river beds and mountains of gold, red, and brown rock. This was the Arabian desert of Sinai, an unending series of monumental rock formations and ever-changing shapes of arid mountains. This is the landscape in which the Greek Orthodox monastery of St. Catherine stands. It was built in the sixth century, at the foot of Mount Sinai where Moses is said to have received the tablets of the Ten Commandments.

Having left the interior to head in the direction of the Gulf of Suez, we flew over Feiran oasis with its abundance of green palms. It looked like a mirage. We finally arrived back on the west coast of Sinai and headed toward Cairo, passing over

Suez, where the canal connects the Mediterranean to the Red Sea. By the time we reached Cairo it was dark. I closed my eyes and once again saw the reefs, the waves, and the fingers of desert that point out into the sea.

At the beginning of November I was in Luxor, or rather ancient Thebes, a fascinating and still mysterious place. I had to concentrate on the great temples of the ancient Egyptians that I knew so well. I was ready, but I was not at ease; I was worried about the light, which is fundamental to creating the atmosphere and to wrapping these temples and the Valley of the Kings in a halo of legend.

We started off, unusually, before the sun rose. I was fully prepared. It was still dark as we approached the Nile in the silence that precedes the dawn. Perhaps everyone was still sleeping. It seemed gray but it was a marvelous morning. The air and sky were clear and the moon on the horizon seemed a good omen. It was cold and I had put on a heavy jacket; the air beat around my face almost to contrast the immobility of the gray countryside in front of me.

Suddenly I noticed that the hills of western Thebes in the distance were taking on a rosy hue and I began to shoot, then I looked around and saw the sun just above the horizon behind me. I had only a few minutes left to photograph with the best of the light. I asked the pilot to head for Deir al-Bahari and the Valley of the Kings.

A moment later we had arrived and in front of me was a sight I shall never forget: the desert had turned pink, orange . . . how can I put it into words? I began to shoot: Deir al-Bahari, the Valley of the Kings with its pyramidal mountain, Deir al-Bahari again, and once more the Valley of the Kings. Three to four minutes had passed and the marvelous light had given way to another—still beautiful, but not magical.

It was 6 a.m. We continued over the temples of Medinet Habu, the Ramesseum, the temple of Seti I, and over the Colossi of Memnon, which are the last remains of the temple of Amenhotep III. We returned toward the Nile to photograph the temples of Luxor and Karnak, the latter being the most majestic in all of ancient Egypt. Columns, courts, pools, sphinxes, and obelisks passed before the viewfinder, reminders of a glorious past still capable of making us wonder.

In the afternoon we headed south along the shores of the Nile, that most mysterious of rivers. It winds like a great serpent through the desert, flanked by fertile land, alone

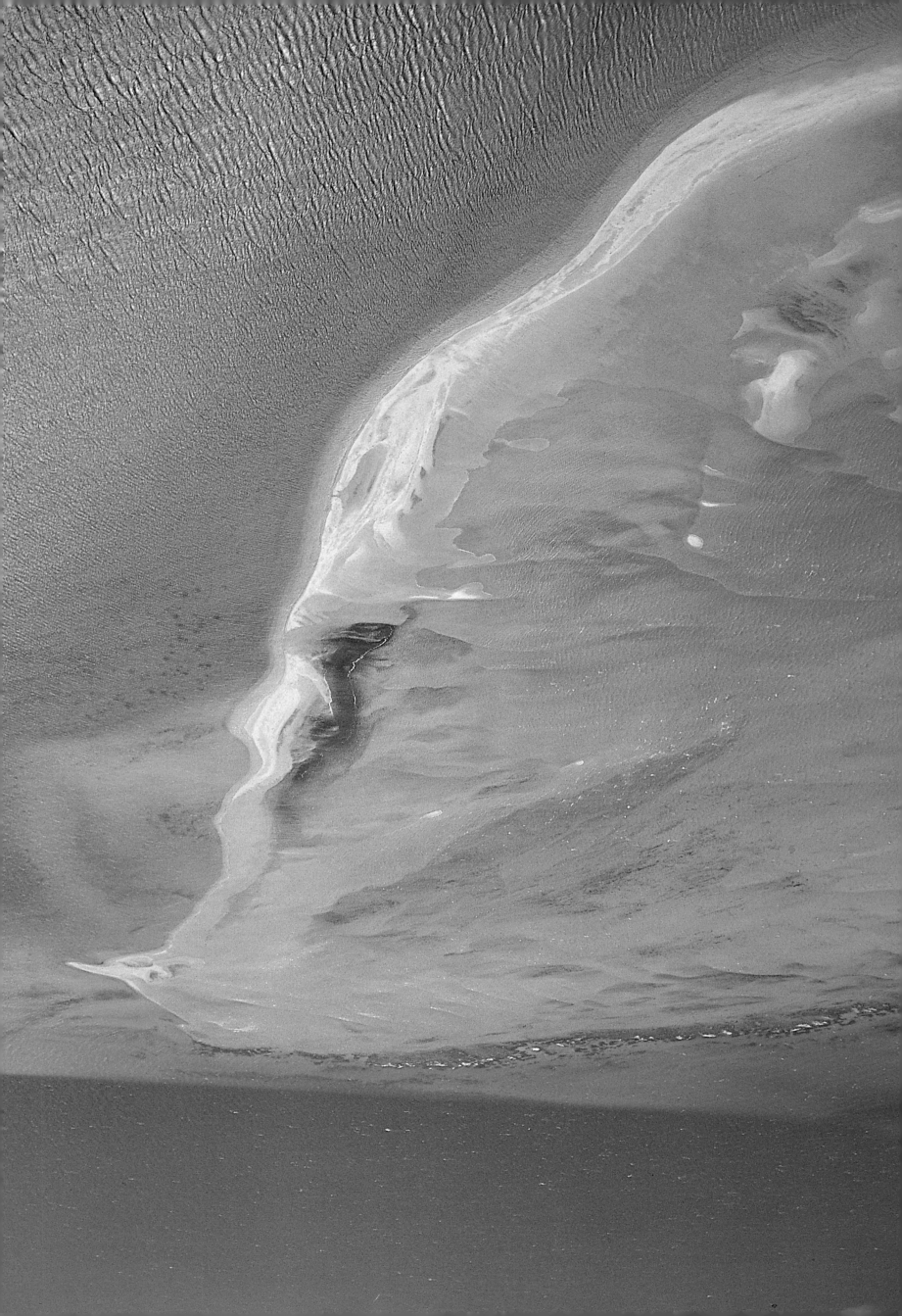

kilometers. I have seen where the Nile begins in Lake Victoria in Uganda, I have admired its twisting course after Murchison Falls, its deep gorges in Ethiopia, and the slow blending of the pale and dark waters of the White and Blue Niles in Khartoum; I have followed its route through Sudan and touched the pyramids of Meroe, the temples in Nubia, the monuments in Thebes, and the pyramids in Giza, and I have studied the civilizations that have grown up along its banks, their histories, and the wars fought to conquer the land. I have always been fascinated by the explorers and missionaries who for centuries searched for the source of the Nile; it was only in 1874 that the secret was discovered. My hero is Henry Stanley, the most courageous of them all.

Finally, this famous river finds peace in the waters of the Mediterranean, almost seeming to want to unite the history of Africa with that of the classical civilizations. As these thoughts passed through my mind, I was studying its winding course through the fields and irrigation canals. Then, in the distance, I saw colored patches of red, yellow, green, and light blue water; these were decanting wells that created an enormous painter's palette of colors in the middle of the brackish lagoon. I took many shots. It was a unique, unexpected, and amazing sight.

We moved on to the marshes of Lake Manzala near the Mediterranean coast to the east of Damietta where, among the greenery of the reeds and rushes, I saw thousands of sailboats, rowboats, and motorboats. The people in them watched me and waved, and I waved back. They seemed happy, stood up in their boats and shouted; I was happy to be there too, in the air but close to them and to their lives, which, for a moment, I was part of. We were obliged to return to Alexandria and I had to leave my new-found friends, the Nile, and my reveries, but I shall never forget them.

The last part of my helicopter wanderings was dedicated to the Libyan desert and its oases, the eastern extreme of the Sahara. Siwa is the most beautiful oasis, like a green and carpet laid down in the desert. It was here that Alexander the Great came to know his divine fate and here, according to tradition, that the great general was buried. The green palms mingle with the calm blue water in a mirage made real.

Ancient ruins remind us of the long history of the oasis and its importance as a junction of the caravan routes that cross the Sahara.

Farther north lies Bahariya, dug out of the desert surface, where large groves of palms break up the arid expanse. The leading Egyptian Egyptologist, Zahi Hawass, has been excavating a necropolis here since 1999 containing thousands of richly adorned mummies from the Late Period. Now the area is known as the Valley of the Golden Mummies.

By now it was late afternoon and we landed in the yard of the elementary school, where a crowd of youngsters and curious bystanders had been waiting for us since morning, as though we were arriving from outer space. They encircled me very quietly and welcomed me with large smiles.

The next day provided me with the most extraordinary sight of my life: the White Desert. We left Bahariya while everyone was still sleeping and headed for the oasis of Farafra. The desert is furrowed by waves of dunes that never seem to cease. The low, skimming light of dawn perfectly emphasized their shapes and colors when, quite unexpectedly, I was presented with a vision that literally took my breath away: the red rocks and pale, fine sand were suddenly interrupted by an immensity of white limestone rocks. Farther ahead, the whiteness covered almost all the desert as if a snowfall had frozen there forever. It was a unique sight. The colors blurred in my viewfinder as I searched for angles and images that could capture my feelings. It was quite simply the most incredible landscape I had ever seen.

And with this image my trip in Egypt came to an end. It is quite needless to say that I will always carry thousands of extraordinary pictures in my mind, or to mention that Egypt has deeply entered my heart, with its matchless, incredibly varied landscapes, its friendly people, and its unique history.

18 The Nile near Lake Manzala creates a dramatic lagoon landscape dominated by hues of vivid green.

20-21 Between al-Mansura and Damietta in the eastern Delta, the Nile winds among bright plots of cultivated land and irrigation channels.

22-23 Western Thebes: the temples of Mentuhotep Nebhepetra and Hatshepsut at Deir al-Bahari. The Valley of the Kings in the background is where the royal tombs of the New Kingdom were constructed.

24-25 The reefs off Hurghada are among the most densely populated in the Egyptian Red Sea and offer a view of an incredible variety of corals and fish at just a few meters' depth.

26-27 Like waves on the sea, the sand dunes that stretch between the oases of Bahariya and Farafra follow hard on each other's heels.

Egypt: Land of Constrast

by Maria Sole Croce

The river that made the long-lasting civilization of ancient Egypt possible appears as a long cobalt blue line winding through fields of bright green and deserts of burning gold. A fertile and beneficent god to the ancient Egyptians, today the Nile is still the essence of the country, the pulsing vein that nourishes the rapidly expanding population by means of a network of increasingly sophisticated irrigation works that fan out to the local level. For 6,500 kilometers, from its Ethiopian and East African sources to its outlet on the Mediterranean, the longest river in the world perpetuates its living force, following the course first laid down by the gods at the time of the creation but now regulated by man to meet his needs.

The banks bathed by Egypt's lifeblood dissolve into landscapes of exquisite beauty transfigured by the sunlight, depending on the time of day and the alternation of the seasons, in a sequence of changing colors as though on a theater stage. The fiery sands of Nubia and the lush flatlands of the Delta are separated by over 1,000 kilometers of desert, highlands, wadis (dried ancient riverbeds), splotches of vegetation, and broad swathes of cultivated land.

To the west of the fertile valley, the highlands of the Libyan Desert feature rocky formations of various types and morphology: the endless expanse of sand is draped over hills, spurs of black pyrite, and smooth masses of white gypsum, seemingly distributed by divine whim in the immense sandy ocean that forms the eastern edge of the Sahara. Here, where the sun is the absolute master and the wind one's only companion, life is concentrated in the five oases: Siwa, Bahariya, Farafra, Dakhla, and Kharga, which have been places of rest and refreshment to armies, caravans, and explorers since man's first appearance here.

To the east, between the Nile and the Red Sea, the panorama has a different appearance: a huge rocky plateau known as the Eastern Desert rises progressively as it stretches towards the seashore, at times reaching heights of over 2,000 meters. Over millions of years, rivers (now no longer existent) dug out deep wadis that join the Nile Valley to the coastal areas, creating natural routes for traders traveling to Arabia, the Sinai peninsula, and the African coast of the Red Sea. It was the precious mineral resources found in this harsh landscape that formed the basis of ancient Egypt's wealth, for in the heart of the eastern and southeastern mountains, there are deposits of gold-bearing quartz from which the "divine" metal was extracted in abundance. Gold was considered to be the incorruptible flesh of the gods who gave man immortality and the country economic supremacy. Beds of emerald, amethyst, and carnelian—mainly in the Nubian regions—supplied the royal court with precious stones while copper, turquoise, and malachite were mined in Sinai.

Modern trade follows other routes; with the opening of the Suez Canal in 1869, the ancient caravan routes were abandoned in favor of sea traffic between the Mediterranean and the Red Sea. The economic benefit to Egypt is clear when one considers that this masterpiece of modern engineering is the only sea route to eastern Africa and the Arabian peninsula from the Mediterranean and Europe without having to circle Africa itself. The political consequences are equally important and Egypt has gained stature in the eyes of the industrialized West—and particularly within the Arab countries—that has raised it to the rank of mediator in the inextricable conflict that lacerates the Middle East.

The other monumental hydraulic work that has changed the face of Egypt is the Aswan High Dam, built in 1964. This was a huge step toward rational exploitation of the Nile's potential, made imperative by a combination of factors: the dizzying demographic increase of roughly one million people a year that was simply incompatible with the surface area of cultivatable land available, and the fact that harvests were constantly threatened by large and unforeseeable variations in the annual flooding of the Nile. Against this background should be set the limited production of the country, which has marginal industrial output.

Thanks to the new dam, Egypt's arable land has been increased by 30% and the building of hydroelectric stations means energy can be sold to neighboring countries. On the other hand, the hydro-geological balance of the entire Nile Valley and Delta has been compromised. The era during which Egypt could be considered the gift of the Nile has ended.

For the ancients, the Nile was the "origin of the world." The river's first flood brought with it fertile silt which it deposited before gently withdrawing, leaving a primordial hill behind it. On this island of mud, the cosmic egg hatched and the sun god, in the form of a bird, took flight and lit up the Earth on its first morning. From this moment, time could be calculated, space could be measured, light rent the darkness, and all that was not came into being. The miracle of the "First Time" was repeated

each day with the rising of the sun and each year by the fertile renewal of the flood, and would continue until the end of the world. Consequently, a cyclical and linear understanding of earthly existence developed, an existence to which only the sun god Atum could put an end by returning all that was created to the muddy waters.

And Atum's prophecy has in part come true. With the construction of the Aswan High Dam and the creation of the artificial lake named after the president of the time, Gamal Abd al-Nasser, the flow of the Nile and its generous cargo of silt was halted. The father of Egypt was imprisoned by his sons and what used to be Lower Nubia (and a good part of Upper Nubia now in Sudan) has been swallowed up by the lake along with many villages and temples and much history. It was only the intervention of UNESCO and the combined efforts of many countries that the most important temples were saved: Philae, Abu Simbel, Kalabsha, and seven other magnificent sacred complexes were separated into pieces, removed, and reconstructed stone by stone on higher ground nearby, a memento of a glorious past that the imperatives of progress had condemned to oblivion.

Nonetheless, the proportion of Egypt that is cultivatable is no more than 6% of the entire country, mainly represented by the northern section of the river valley, the Delta, the larger oases, and the narrow northern coastal strip. This is too little for a population of 65 million, the second highest in Africa after Nigeria, which is in constant growth. There are few cities of any size and, with the exception of Alexandria and the megalopolis of Cairo, they do not exceed 400,000 inhabitants. They are much more like urbanized villages that have exploded during the last few decades, centered around the growth in tourism and the construction of new industrial plants. Most of them lie in the Delta, while to the south it is on the river banks that the population lives. The river and the monuments of the ancient civilization are the driving forces behind the huge business of tourism, which succeeds in creating wealth even in environmentally less favored areas. However, the economic and social benefits that have followed from the modernization of society (for example, increasing literacy and female emancipation) have affected only the privileged minority.

Mud houses close to farming and industrial areas and far from the tourist tracks are evidence of communities where life is a daily struggle and survival is not to be taken for granted. In many areas, clean water supplies are still lacking despite the efforts made to improve the irrigation and drainage systems. This is a reminder that the million square kilometers that form the territory of Egypt are simply a portion of the immense desert that runs across Africa from the Atlantic to the Red Sea.

Nevertheless, the desert has substantial economic potential. Far from the Nile in the western desert, there lie extensive deposits of "black gold": today, Egypt is one of the largest exporters of oil and other raw materials, but the costs—particularly in terms of ecological compatibility—are high.

The impact of technological and industrial progress is major, especially for a country in which nature often exists in pure, unspoilt beauty. Delicate biological balances have been compromised by the construction of the High Dam and the Suez Canal and to these effects must be added the infrastructures required to welcome annually the millions of tourists that represent the country's major source of income.

The most significant instance is to be seen where the wedge of Sinai pushes into the sea to create the gulfs of Aqaba and Suez and on the Red Sea coast of the mainland down to the sandy beaches of Qusayr to the south of Hurghada, the ancient port from which the pharaohs' ships sailed on their trips to the land of Punt, thought to be between the modern countries of Eritrea and Somalia, to supply the kingdom with gold, ebony, ivory, incense, and highly prized oils. Incomparable for its wealth of flora and fauna, the Red Sea is ideal for sub-aqua enthusiasts. The lovely, well-equipped beaches are visited each year by 200,000 tourists in search of sun, sea, and exoticism, and their expectations are not disappointed. Over the last twenty years, this area has undergone intense development that has often been incompatible with protection of the natural environment, with the result that the authorities have created protected areas like the marvelous Ras Muhammad National Marine Park on the southern tip of Sinai.

This is the reality of Egypt, a land of strong contrasts that draws on a cultural inheritance that has no equal in the world. The myth and the reality coexist in a dimension that is partly accessible, partly out of reach; ancient and modern share the same soil without ever really merging, yet their complementariness succeeds in giving a tangible sense to the ancestral history of Egypt.

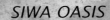

Marsa Matruh

al-Alamein

SIWA OASIS

BAHARIYA OASIS

FARAFRA OASIS

WESTERN
DESERT

DAKHLA OASIS

30 top
The Mediterranean
coast between
al-Alamein and
Sidi Abd al-Rahman.

30 bottom The ruins of
old Siwa and, in the
background, the
limestone hills that frame
Lake Siwa.

32-33 Luxor,
the famous "hundred-
gated Thebes,"
is a pleasant town
on the Nile.
The Libyan highlands
above the cultivated
strip of land are where
the Theban
necropolises lie.

36-37 The desert
embraces a large Muslim
cemetery that lies in the
shadow of the pyramids
at Saqqara, near the
village of the same name.

38-39 The underwater
geography of the wide
bay off Marsa Matruh is
reflected in the changing
colors of the
Mediterranean; the shore
offers clean and well-
equipped beaches that
are visited by many
tourists in the summer.

34-35 The date palm
plantations at Siwa turn
the oasis into an
immense ocean of green
in the middle of the
desert.

ROSETTA
Baltim
DAMIETTA
Lake Manzala
ALEXANDRIA
PORT SAID
al-Mahalla
al-Mansura
al-Arish
Damanhur
Zifta
SUEZ CANAL
Zagazig
ISMAILIYA

SUEZ
SINAI
PENINSULA
GIZA
CAIRO
Saqqara
Dahshur
Taba
LAKE QARUN
FAYOUM
Meidum
GULF OF SUEZ
*MONASTERY OF
ST. ANTHONY*
Nuweiba
Kom
*MONASTERY OF
ST. PAUL*
*MONASTERY OF
ST. CATHERINE*
Medinet Madi
Beni Suef
Tebtynis
*MONASTERY OF
ST. SAMUEL*
Dahab
SHARM
AL-SHEIKH
TIRAN
al-Minya
EASTERN DESERT
Straits of Gubal
RAS MUHAMMAD

Gulf of Aqaba

HURGHADA

Asyut

RED SEA

PORT SAFAGA

Abydos
Qusayr

Dendera

*VALLEY OF THE KINGS
WESTERN THEBES*
KARNAK
LUXOR

KHARGA OASIS
Esna

Edfu
Wadi Gimal I.

KOM OMBO

ASWAN
TEMPLE OF PHILAE
Aswan High Dam

RAS BANAS

*LAKE
NASSER*

Wadi al-Sebua

Abu
Simbel

31

The Delta and the Mediterranean Coast

The fertile plain that fans out toward the Mediterranean is the last gift of the Nile before its waters flow into the sea. A few miles north of Cairo, where the placid and majestic river forks into the two large Rosetta and Damietta branches, the land undergoes an unexpected metamorphosis and opens to form a huge green expanse veined by scores of canals.

This is the Delta, the luxuriant tip of Lower Egypt, formed by the accumulation of alluvial deposits transported by the Nile on its way to the sea. Over tens of thousands of years, the huge Mediterranean gulf that washed up against the area of Cairo was progressively filled with layers of mud and river detritus until it was transformed into what is today the green lung of Egypt, edged to the north by a ragged lace of white beaches. The extraordinary fertility of the land—once inhospitable—is the generous gift of the continuous labor of the farmers and, above all, of the many irrigation works that were carried out by the authorities from the first half of the nineteenth century to improve the benefits offered by the Nile. It was the famous Muhammad Ali Pasha who in 1835 completed the barrages on the Rosetta and Damietta branches that had been planned by Napoleon to regulate irrigation of the Delta and facilitate their navigation. Later, many other projects were carried out to increase farming productivity and to expand the arable surface area until the High Dam was completed in 1964. Even today, the urgent need to find new land to feed the growing number of people has stimulated continuous hydro-geological projects, also involving the Suez Canal, to irrigate new land.

The appearance of the land was very different when Alexander the Great arrived as conqueror and, in 332 BCE, placed the first stone in the construction of Alexandria. *Tamehw* ("the land of papyrus plants") to the ancient Egyptians was no more than an expanse of marshes and clumps of papyrus teeming with aquatic life that reflected the state of the world as it emerged from the mud during the Creation. In this primordial habitat, the slender, elegant stems and fluffy flowers of the papyrus groves mingled with the shady reeds in which the goddess Isis hid to bring up her son Horus in secret. Hunting water birds in these marshy lands was one of the most popular pastimes of ancient princes and

dignitaries, who could penetrate the dense vegetation on their manoeuvrable boats made from strips of knotted papyrus stems. Adopted as the heraldic emblem of northern Egypt, the noble papyrus was often associated with the lotus flower, which was the political symbol of Upper (southern) Egypt; the two plants combined represented the union of the Two Lands over which the pharaohs exercised absolute sovereignty.

The softest fibers of the flexible stem of the papyrus were used to make the soft and resistant writing material which took its name from the plant. But the progressive reclamation of the marshes and the more recent industrial settlements have completely checked the spontaneous growth of this long-established umbrellifer and it survives only in the man-made environments of botanical gardens.

A meeting point for northeast Africa, Mediterranean Europe, and Asia Minor, Lower Egypt played a fundamental role in the formation of the pharaonic civilization; it complemented development in the south of the country, although there are far fewer archaeological remains to be seen. The magnificent reminders of the past, preserved in Upper Egypt by the dry and salubrious climate of the deserts, have almost disappeared here, swallowed by the deposits of alluvial silt that have been carried into the Delta over the millennia. In such conditions, an essential aid in archaeological research has been surveying from the air. Aerial photography allows one to see features not visible from the ground and renders them permanent on film. Exposure to light from different angles can bring out slight variations in the soil, depending on how long and thick the vegetation is and how damp it may be. This in turn can reflect the presence of buried structures such as walls, channels, roads, water tanks, tombs, etc. Of course, for practical reasons, it is not always possible to excavate in agricultural or urban areas, so the temples, palaces, and cities, that were at one time sumptuous capitals, flourishing trading centers, and multi-ethnic crossroads of the ancient world still mostly remain buried beneath villages and cultivated fields.

Paradoxically, it is in these country areas so bereft of archaeological monuments and unvisited by tourists that the

41 A sailing boat on the largest lake in the Delta, Lake Manzala, which is separated from the Mediterranean by a narrow strip of land.

authentic spirit of the Egypt of the past can still be seen. The rural landscape of orchards and fields is not only an idyllic picture but a trip through time to a world suspended between the past and the present. Here the activities of farmers, shepherds, and small agricultural communities remain almost unaltered from the ancient times when they fed themselves, the court, and the temples.

Almost as though it had been passed over by technological progress, rural life in the Delta is the same as can be seen in the lively realism of the wall paintings in ancient Egyptian tombs: silent feluccas gliding over the canals, fragrant eucalyptus and palm groves laden with fruit, *fellahin* cultivating the fields using the same methods as their ancestors, and the shouts of children mingling with the sounds of the village animals. The *shaduf*, the most common and traditional means of drawing water, operates between the fields, and oxen are used to plow the fields where the farmer's hoe cannot reach. Irrigated by a dense network of canals, the land is a patchwork of different colors depending on what is growing on it: wheat, rice, maize, cotton, clover, and a great variety of fruit and vegetables together form a bucolic tapestry of great beauty.

The atmosphere on the Delta coast is quite different. The coast is a strip 200 kilometers long of bays, lagoons, deep inlets, and white beaches. Narrow bands of sand separate large lakes from the sea, for example, lakes Maryut, Burullus, and Manzala, where the sons of Amun-Ra once grew vines but which are now homes to herons and flamingos.

These were the departure points of the trading and military routes between ancient Egypt and the Mediterranean basin. The ramifications of the Nile fostered busy trade within the Delta and increased the number of means of access to the sea; the outlets of the main distributaries (ancient sources refer to at least five, but today there are only two, Rosetta and Damietta) were natural channels suitable for the berthing and departure of ships. The superb fleets of the pharaohs were always on the move with cargos of stone, wood, gifts, and tributes. They comprised ferries, fishing boats, warships, and merchant ships in a continual flux that,

in addition to goods, exported and imported that most precious of assets, culture.

Progress in underwater archaeology has meant that remains of ancient Egyptian ports have been recovered, particularly in the area of Alexandria, where the sea bottom close to the coast has given up blocks of stone and fragments of statues that encourage the slender hope of salvaging, if not the famous lighthouse of Pharos, perhaps the ancient buildings in the Hellenistic city.

With the passage of time, the various ports knew alternating periods of glory and decline in their continual contest for supremacy over the military and commercial sea traffic but, as a result of the secular historical and geological processes experienced, there is no trace of the other ancient Egyptian ports on the seabed close to the coast.

Alexandria, the country's largest port today, experienced temporary decline during the eighth to the ninth centuries to the benefit of the nearby city of Rashid (Rosetta), founded by the Arabs in 870 on the ruins of an older city. The revival of Alexandria under Muhammad Ali Pasha notably reduced the economic and political importance of its rival port, and the modern Rosetta remains a pleasant town, Ottoman in style, crossed by palm-lined avenues onto which the mosaics and inlays of the old mosques and caliphs' palaces face. It was at the St. Julien Fort near this town that Captain Bouchard of the Napoleonic forces found the famous Rosetta Stone that allowed Jean-François Champollion to decipher Egyptian hieroglyphic writing.

The history of Damietta (ancient Tamiathis) was decidedly stormier; today it is only a small center for coastal trade but it was at one time, especially after Arab occupation, a prosperous town for merchants dealing in coffee, rice, oil, and dates. Situated in a strategic position on the northeast coast, it was the setting for ferocious battles—with alternating outcomes—between the Crusaders and the Arabs until its fortress was finally destroyed in 1251 and rebuilt farther west by the Mamluk sultan Baybars. More recently, the building of the Suez Canal and consequent rise in importance of Port Said eclipsed Damietta's commercial importance and today the town is mostly supported by small

industries associated with the agricultural activity in the Delta.

Indeed, all the northeastern area of the Delta has been heavily affected by the presence of the canal that connects the Red Sea to the Mediterranean. Without this massive engineering work, the sandy region that forms the natural boundary with Sinai would have remained what it had been for millennia: arid and desolate land of no interest to anyone except for commercial or military traffic between Egypt and the Middle East. There were no cities, temples, or villages in the desert, just small tribes of Bedouin and bands of bandits that preyed on the caravan routes. This area was the point of passage for Asian peoples invading Egypt in the past: the armies of the Hyksos, Assyrians, Persians, and Arabs trod these routes, but the dust of time has wiped out every trace of their passing.

It is a fact that the history of Suez coincides with the history of modern Egypt. The opening of the canal in 1869 was a sensational event that inaugurated a new era for the economic life of the country, enabling settlements in previously uninhabitable territories thanks to the creation of ports whose importance would grow in parallel to the flow of sea traffic.

The execution of the ambitious project that had been laid down by the progressive Muhammad Said Pasha was completed by his son Ismail after years of hard work and innumerable political obstacles to be overcome. The enterprise was extremely costly to Egypt, which was obliged to turn to Europe for the required financing and technologies. France made a large though not disinterested contribution, which it wanted repaid as a sort of political protectorate shared with Britain that lasted until 1956.

The account written by Herodotus, borne out by archaeological remains, informs us that a navigable passage between the Nile and the Red Sea already existed in antiquity. The force behind this project was probably the Saite pharaoh Nekau II who, in the seventh century BCE, diverted the Pelusiac branch of the river near Bubastis by channeling the water into the dried out bed of the Wadi Tumilat as far as Lake Timsah, where the city of Ismailia now stands. From

here, ships were able to reach the gulf by crossing the various connected Bitter Lakes. The remains of the canals are still visible at certain points in the region.

In relation to this canal, aerial photography once again showed itself to be of major value for archaeological reconstruction. Reconnaissance carried out by the Israeli air force in 1975 discovered the presence of the ancient canal that joined the Gulf of Suez to the Mediterranean. Flying over the area to the west of Ismailia, it is possible to see the remains of the site of Tjeku, the "House of Atum" near the modern Tell al-Maskhuta, which was the only rest stop on the middle section of Wadi Tumilat.

Just a few miles from Tjeku, but constructed 2,500 years later, the modern town of Ismailia was the most elegant to be built along the banks of the canal during the period the works were in progress. The graceful villas that line the flowery walks of the center are reminiscent of a *fin de siècle* colonial town designed in the style of the Europeans who worked here for Khedive Ismail. The gardens and trees that surround the port are reflected in the blue water of Lake Timsah, the smallest of the Bitter Lakes, which lies two thirds of the way down the canal. Although its name means "Crocodile Lake," no such creatures inhabit its waters and its banks are lined with superb beaches and many bathing areas. Fed by many natural springs, the area around the town is a green belt speckled with the bright colors of tomatoes, mangoes, and strawberries.

Leaving the canal and flying over the central eastern section of the Delta, the immense verdant plain seems infinite. From time to time, the eye is attracted by some hill that breaks the flatness; these are referred to as *tell (or kom)*, artificial mounds formed over the centuries by the accumulation of once-inhabited, ancient structures. Found in isolated nuclei or piled on larger surfaces, often half-buried by crops or villages, these masses of ruins are the only vestiges of an ancient past. What remained after the arrival of the Arabs—who dismantled magnificent pharaonic monuments to build their own palaces and mosques in Cairo—was demolished by local farmers in a search for *sebbakh*, a material rich in fertilizing elements found in decomposing mud bricks.

The tourist in search of spectacular monuments will be disappointed by the poor quality of pharaonic ruins in the Delta, because this is the other side of Egypt, where humans of every level are massed as they struggle through the ineluctable transitoriness of earthly life. Yet a certain appeal emanates from these places betrayed by history, as though voices from the past call out on the wind to remind us that here, in eras long past, the great capitals of Lower Egypt once stood with their temples, maze-like necropolises, and catacombs. Over the past few decades, the efforts of archaeologists in the Delta have produced miracles in the attempt to give substance and dignity to the sparse remains that lie on the ground; although there were no elevated sections left, it has been possible to understand their original constructions and the transformations the ancient settlements have undergone. A view from the sky aids in making sense of the apparent disorder of the ruins. As one rises from the ground, the ancient layout can be made out: the perimeter of the defensive walls, the columns of the porticoes, the empty areas that were the gardens, and the foundations of the houses; all these elements contribute to reconstruct the image of the original setting.

An area measuring 10 kilometers between Tell al-Dab'a and Qantir on the Pelusiac branch of the Nile was the site of the famous city of Avaris where the Asiatic invaders, the Hyksos, settled to govern Egypt during the Fifteenth Dynasty (1650–1550 BCE). Later, the Ramessid pharaohs turned the city into a magnificent royal residence named Pi-Ramesses. Saved from agricultural and urban expansion, excavation of the site is still underway: it appears like an enormous mosaic that Egyptologists are trying to piece together.

Many monuments that originally adorned the city have been found on a site a little to the north, at Tanis, which was the capital and burial place of the pharaohs of the Twenty-first and Twenty-second Dynasties (1075–718 BCE) and, until the end of the pharaonic epoch, the largest and most powerful city in the Delta. Following a practice that was fairly common in ancient Egypt, the Tanite sovereigns took many statues, obelisks, sphinxes, and other architectural elements from their predecessors and reused them to embellish their own, newly built residence.

In the center of this vast plain free of all vegetation, the ruins of Tanis lie on a *tell* beneath a sky that is often low and cloudy in an almost surreal and lunar atmosphere. Rare dust-covered statues replaced on their feet stand like ghosts among the hundreds of colossal blocks that lie on the ground in desolate confusion. Seen from the sky, the great *temenos* that housed the temple of Amun and the other religious complexes can be seen in all its poignant transience and the echo of its past greatness fades among the stones strewn, seemingly haphazardly, on the ground. For a while, the silver on the sarcophaguses and the gold on the beautiful grave goods found in the royal necropolis discovered to the south of the temple lit up the gloomy atmosphere of Tanis, but the dazzle of these objects was soon transferred to the Egyptian Museum in Cairo.

The ruins of Bubastis, Sais, Naukratis, Buto, and the other great political and religious centers of Lower Egypt have not received a kinder fate. Like the noble lineages that shared in their past glories, they suffered a slow decline that has resulted today in piles of rubble, but the appeal emitted by the ruins scattered among the countryside is one of the most intense feelings the Delta can offer to the visitor.

The situation in Alexandria is different; Alexandria is the only city to have perpetuated its ancient tradition to the present day. Situated on the rocky isthmus between the sea and Lake Maryut, the modern city is a thin strip that extends for 20 kilometers along the coast. Flying over the surrounding region, signs of the old canals that connected Alexandria with the Canopic branch of the Nile can still be seen. These were ingenious navigable channels that allowed trade between the Delta, the Nile Valley, and the Mediterranean.

The oldest remains in the city date to at least one century before the arrival of the great Macedonian general, who founded the second capital of his empire here, transforming the small Egyptian port of Rhakotis into the most brilliant and cosmopolitan metropolis in the Mediterranean. As the political and commercial hub of Hellenistic and Roman Egypt, Alexandria was a melting pot of different cul-

tures and religions, among them the large Jewish community. In an intellectual ferment that has no parallel in ancient history, eastern and western traditions came together and enriched one another, bringing to life cultural institutions, libraries, and academies that for centuries attracted the most illustrious philosophers and thinkers.

With the advent of Christianity, the pagan roots of Alexandria were the first to submit to the new doctrine. Having always been receptive to the most diverse ideas, the city evangelized by St. Mark around 40 CE played a decisive role in the spreading of Christianity throughout Egypt and participated in the lively theological disputes that divided the early church. The patriarchs of Alexandria opted in the end for complete autonomy, adopting the monophysite doctrine and founding the Coptic church. Monasteries and hermitages sprang up in the deserts that ran along either side of the Nile Valley and small Coptic communities were established which, until the fourth century CE, were ferociously persecuted by the Roman emperors. The monasteries of Wadi Natrun to the southeast of Alexandria, those of St. Anthony and St. Paul close to the Red Sea, and that of St. Catherine in Sinai were the interpreters and custodians of the ancient Christian traditions in Egypt. But the bloody persecution meted out upon the Egyptian heretics racked the country to the point that when the Persians invaded in 619 CE they were welcomed by the population, if not with enthusiasm, at least with relief.

During the Arab occupation, Alexandria's development was brought to a sudden and long halt. Trade with the east had been the city's primary source of wealth and, despite this having been harmed during the ruinous years of political and religious troubles, under the Arabs trade was dramatically reduced to the benefit of the city's new capital, Cairo.

For the Queen of the Mediterranean, it was the start of a long decline. When Napoleon disembarked there with his army of soldiers and the two hundred scientists in his retinue, he found little more than a fishing village. It was only in the nineteenth century with the longsighted ambitions of Muhammad Ali Pasha that dignity and prestige were restored to the geographically favored city, and Alexandria once more became a flourishing port and cosmopolitan city popular with the aristocracies of Egypt and Europe.

Modern Alexandria has maintained much of the elegant architecture and atmosphere of that period but the remains of its classical past have all but disappeared beneath the foundations of modern buildings. All that is left is the splendid Roman theater, the ruins of the baths, and the slender column that stands as the last remnant of the ancient temple of Serapis. Incorrectly named "Pompey's Pillar," it was in fact raised by Diocletian.

On the eastern tip of the promontory that separates the two main ports and where the imposing fifteenth-century fort of Qaytbay stands, there was an island where one of the seven wonders of the ancient world once stood, the great lighthouse that for one thousand years was the radiant symbol of Alexandria. On the western tip, a large esplanade of gardens is the site of the old royal residence of Ras al-Tin that was built by Muhammad Ali Pasha and inhabited by the rulers of Egypt until 1952, when Egypt ceased being a monarchy and became the first independent Arab republic.

Farther west, the aerial view of the coastal strip emphasizes the neat contrast between the clear turquoise waters of the Mediterranean and the string of tourist facilities that face onto the beaches. 105 kilometers along the coast, the visitor's emotions are aroused at al-Alamein, the site of the bloodiest battle for control of North Africa during World War II. In October 1942, the Allied army under Field Marshal Montgomery attacked and decisively defeated the Italian and German troops led by Field Marshal Rommel, but tens of thousands were left dead on the battlefield.

The three large war cemeteries that lie just outside the town are a stirring expanse of graves and cenotaphs that dramatically convey the extent of the sacrifice of life. *They lacked fortune, not courage"* is the moving epitaph to the Italian dead built on the road that leads to the memorial, and it is in the name of that courage and the ideals that bolstered it that the white stones bleaching beneath the African sun are so profound and tragic.

46-47 As it approaches the sea, the eastern arm of the Nile winds in large bends through the cotton plantations that make the area between al-Mansura and Damietta one of the wealthiest in the rural Delta.

48-49 and 49 top
Port equipment and
storehouses at the mouth
of the Damietta branch of
the Nile. A series of
breakwaters protects the
coast from the power of

the sea. In ancient times,
when it was not under
attack from Crusaders,
the outlet of the Nile was
filled by merchant ships
carrying coffee, linen, oil,
and dates.

49 bottom Before spilling
into the Mediterranean,
the Nile crosses the green
flatlands of Rosetta, which
were once unhealthy
lagoons but today are
lush plantations.

50 Sailors reconcile
the transportation
of goods with the
requirements of
the daily wash.

51 Sail swollen by the
wind, a boat scuds across
Lake Manzala.

52-53 A view of Lake
Manzala. This is the
largest body of water in
the Delta, still mostly
marshy from the silt
washed here by the
ancient branches of the
Nile.

53 top The small
promontories and marshy
expanses of Lake Manzala
are home to many fish.

53 bottom A group of
underwater fishermen
in a marshy area
of Lake Manzala.

*54 and 55 Navigable
channels through the
marshes of Lake Manzala
in the southern inlet near
al-Matariya. The green
saltwater contrasts with
the brilliant colors of the
islands.*

*56-57 The narrow
arm of the Nile
near Lake Manzala
creates a spectacular
lagoon landscape with
dazzling hues of green
and blue.*

*58-59 Tanks for
mineral extraction
near Damietta glint
in the sun like a mosaic
of colored glass tiles.*

60-61 Donkeys are still the most common means of transport for the fellahin of the Delta. Their rural life seems quite resistant to change. The agricultural economy of Egypt centers on the cultivation of cotton, cereals, and sugar cane.

61 The combination of crop rotation and capillary irrigation have resulted in a substantial increase in cultivatable land. The countryside near Tanta in the western Delta is famous for its cotton, the quality of which is renowned.

62 The lovely town of
Damietta stands on the
right bank of the eastern
branch of the Nile.
At one time it was
a flourishing goods port,
but today it is used for
local coastal navigation.

63 The ancient town of
Rosetta was founded in
the ninth century on the
outlet of the western
branch of the Nile.
It became famous at the
end of the eighteenth
century as the site where
the trilingual stele
known as the Rosetta

Stone was found,
allowing J-.F. Champollion
to decipher the meanings
of the hieroglyphs. The
city lies sixty-five
kilometers east of
Alexandria and was
Egypt's largest port until
the beginning of the
nineteenth century.

64-65 Cultivated fields along one of the many canals near Damanhur, the ancient "City of Horus," today an important farming town that specializes in processing cotton and breeding chickens.

66-67 Cultivation of shellfish on the coast near Damietta. The coastal strip between Damietta and Port Said faces onto the large Lake Manzala, which is separated from the sea by a ribbon of land.

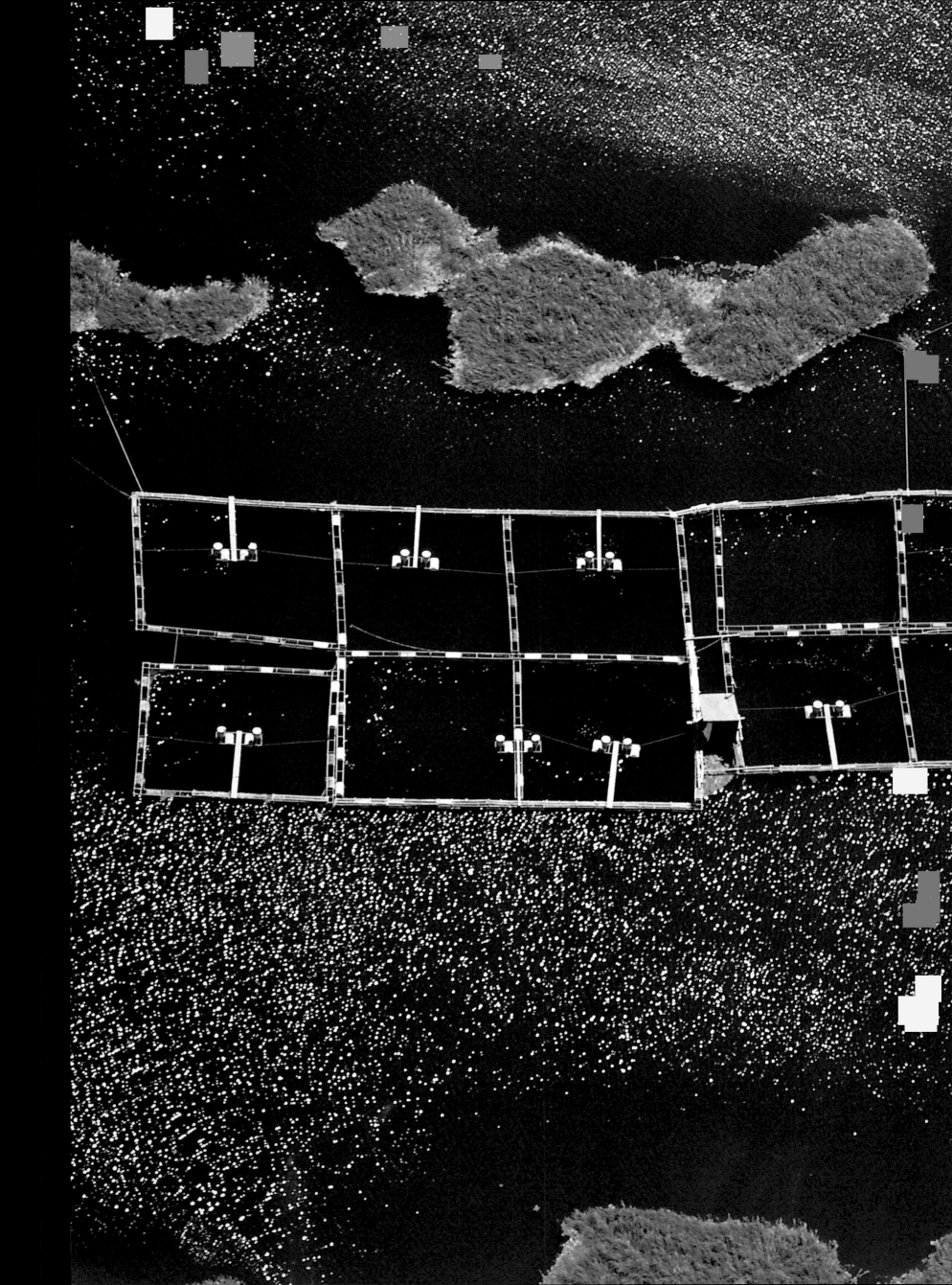

68 and 69 The wreck of a merchant ship that ran aground in the shallows near Abu Qir. It lies half submerged in the area where the fleets of French and British ships fought the Battle of the Nile in 1798.

70-71 The mosque of Abu al-Abbas in Alexandria exemplifies the vigor of modern Islamic architecture. The fort of Sultan Qaytbay stands in the background.

71 top The new Alexandria Library, designed by a group of Norwegian architects. It stands to the east of the city center, and the circular structure is slightly inclined toward the sea.

71 bottom View of the Eastern Harbor in Alexandria with Qaytbay Fort and the Yacht Club. In the background is the Ras al-Tin promontory and the large Western Harbor.

72-73 The fort of Sultan Qaytbay is one of the best preserved examples of the Arab defensive system. It was

built in the fifteenth century on the location where the famous lighthouse of Alexandria once stood.

74-75 The memorial to the German dead at al-Alamein stands a few kilometers from the city. An obelisk stands in the center of the five-sided building.

75 An immaculate tower on the beach at Tell al-Eisa commemorates the Italians who died in 1942 at the battle of al-Alamein. The struggle for control of North Africa ended in victory for the Allied troops, but cost 80,000 lives.

76-77 The coast of
Marsa Matruh alternates
between tongues of sand
and small inlets with low
cliffs.

The ancient lagoon from
which the fleets of
Cleopatra sailed against
Augustus lies to the west
of the port.

77 For over 100
kilometers between
Alexandria and
al-Alamein, the coast is
a long ribbon of tourist
villages and private
residential complexes.

Large swimming
pools and artificial
beaches are integrated
into the natural
coast to satisfy the
dramatic increase
in tourism.

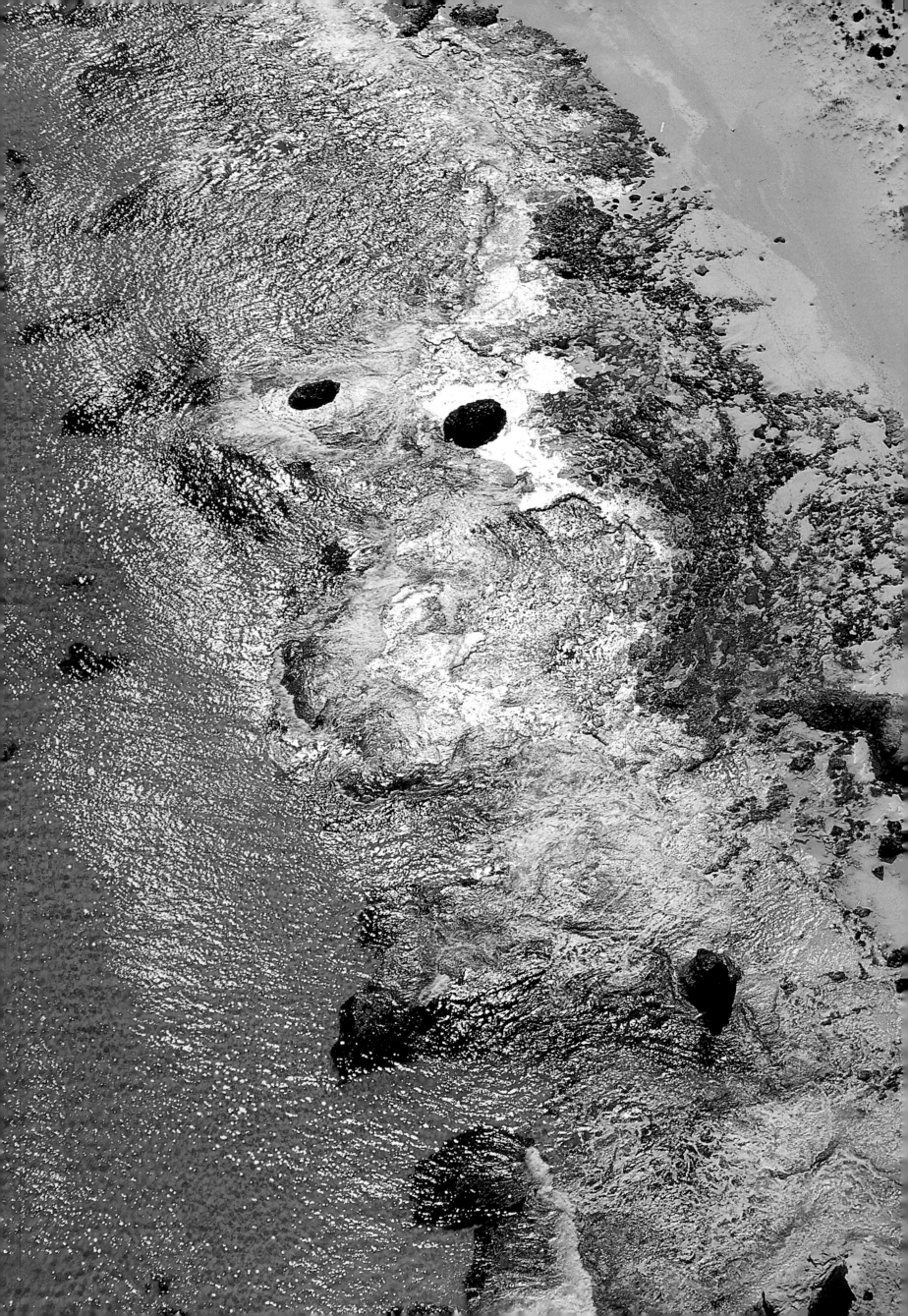

78 and 79
The Mediterranean coast
between al-Alamein and
Sidi Abd al-Rahman has
many untouched beaches
and clear turquoise
water. In some places,
the coastline is broken
up by sand and rocks
that slope gently down
into the sea, at others
by boulders and stones.
80-81 It is not uncommon
near Marsa Matruh to find
completely empty beaches
of fine sand and rocks
that gently break the
surface of the water.

Cairo and the Pyramid Fields

The identification of Islamic Egypt with its capital is profoundly rooted in the historical memory of its people, to the extent that the Arabic word *Misr* is the name not only of the city but of the entire country.

The founding of the city in 640 coincided with the entry of Byzantine Egypt into the Islamic empire. Eight years after the death of Muhammad, the Prophet's second successor—Caliph Omar—decided that the country of birth of one of the Prophet's wives, Maryam the Copt, was to become a province of Islam. As a center for Arab culture (and later for Turkish Ottoman culture) in the Nile Valley, Cairo and Egypt actively experienced the political and religious changes that disturbed the Islamic world until the expansion of European imperialist influence in the nineteenth century and the country's rebirth as an independent nation.

The aerial view of the city is bewildering: all of Arab Egyptian history is written in the architecture of its buildings in an extraordinary amalgam that also incorporates the earlier Christian culture. Stately emblems of the area's pharaonic past lie on the edges of the city: the pyramids of Giza and, a little south, the tombs and temples in the archaeological areas of Saqqara, Abu Sir, and Dahshur, besieged by tourists whose every emotional expectation is fully satisfied.

Anyone who has landed at Cairo airport after dark will know the magical feeling of being immersed in all-enveloping space as the stars in the sky blend with the pinpoints of lights of the city below. The city is so large that, by night, its outer edges merge with the horizon and the sky above.

In the first light of dawn, the city reasserts its physicality, with domed mosques, minarets, and old palaces dominating the twisting alleyways of the old districts. The shops, cafés, and stalls of sweets and fruit that dot the narrow streets soon teem with all kinds of humanity that could come straight out of a story by Naguib Mahfouz.

Perennially in conflict between tradition and progress, Cairo is a modern megalopolis that has perhaps grown up too fast around an ancient, pulsing heart. She is the Mother of the World and is a synopsis of all the contradictions of a country aimed at the future though still solidly anchored to an authoritative and intrinsic past that cannot but affect its present. Just a few kilometers separate the massive modern hotels from the poorer areas on the edge of the city. The streets are filled with exhaust fumes and the incessant clamour of horns and small carts pulled by donkeys, while the broken sidewalks are covered by a river of people who risk their lives every time they try to cross the road. The sweetish smell of the water-pipe, the *shisha*, and the appetizing aroma of kebabs mingle with the infinite odors in the saturated air, not all of them pleasant, with which the twenty million inhabitants seem to live without difficulty. In the tumult of the city and amid the regular rhythms of the calls to prayer by the *muezzin*, only the great father Nile seems calm and indifferent as it slides between the tree-lined banks, where some shade is available when the sun is at its hottest.

The large building that has housed the Museum of Egyptian Antiquities since 1890 stands in the heart of Cairo, in al-Tahrir Square. The museum collection numbers over 100,000 archaeological objects from the pharaonic era without counting what is held in the stores. Inspired by Classical architecture, which at the time was very fashionable, both the interior and exterior of the museum are imbued with an ancient and rather outmoded appeal that matches its surroundings very well.

To the east of the city, the majestic Citadel founded by Saladin in 1176 dominates Cairo from a spur of the Muqattam hills. Since its construction, the Citadel has always been the symbol of the city and the residence of successive Mamluk sultans and Ottoman pashas. At the highest point, Muhammad Ali built the great alabaster mosque whose structure of domes, half-domes and slender minarets is a magnificent example of Turkish Ottoman architecture. From here there is a wonderful view of Cairo at sunset that stretches as far as the Pyramids, while a reddish glow lights up the faded and dusty expanse of roofs below.

At the foot of the hill outside the ancient city walls lies the sandy plain that is home to the City of the Dead, the Mamluk graveyard in which the oldest tombs date from the beginning of the twelfth century. The tombs were designed to be homes for the dead—in Egypt this custom seems to have descended from the pharaonic tradition—that incorporate courtyards, fountains, lodging for the custodian, and even accommodation for visiting relatives. Today these sumptuous tombs are home to thousands of people, many of whom were evacuated from the Canal zone after the defeat of the Six Day War in 1967.

To the west, there is the great mosque of Ibn Tulun, who in 869, after the crumbling of the Islamic empire into various local potentates, occupied Egypt on behalf of the caliph of Baghdad and turned it into his own governorate. One of the country's most successful periods began at that time, thanks to the resumption in manufacture of local products and to a flurry of construction that enlarged the city. Breaking the traditions of its predecessors, the new dynasty moved its residence onto the hill that used to overlook the old city of Fustat from the northeast; this resulted in the building of new districts of great magnificence, of which we are aware only from accounts of the period. Palaces, gardens, baths, and markets were built around the great mosque that today looks down on just another of the many dusty quarters of the city.

Misr al-Fustat is the oldest section of the city. Its remains, currently being excavated, can still be seen in the small area opposite the southern tip of the island of Roda near the Coptic Museum

82 The glinting domes of the mosque of Muhammad Ali, which was built in the first half of the nineteenth century in the center of the medieval Citadel that dominates Cairo.

though they lie scattered among Roman ruins and Coptic, Catholic, and Greek Orthodox churches and cemeteries. The story goes that the district was built in the very spot that the commander of Omar's troops, Amr Ibn al-As, put up his tent (*fustat* in Arabic) when besieging the Byzantine fort known as Babylon; it was the conquest of this fort that signaled the start of the Islamic occupation of the Nile Valley. However much it has been restored, Amr's mosque is the oldest existing Islamic building in Egypt. Fustat grew and prospered as a political and military center under the Umayyad and Abbasid dynasties until the Fatimid rulers (who arrived in 969) created the new capital of al-Qahira ("the Victorious"), a short distance away.

From a colony of Baghdad, Egypt became an independent state. Using luxury and magnificence to boost their prestige, the courts of the Fatimid rulers transformed Cairo into a capital sparkling with marble, ivory, crystal, and gold. The mosque of al-Azhar was built as a symbol of the new Shi'ite doctrine with which the direct descendants of Fatima, the daughter of the Prophet, wanted to reinstall their version of Islam. In the thirteenth century, the Mamluk sultans enriched the mosque with porticoes, gateways, minarets, and libraries to turn it into what soon became one of the largest centers for the study of Qur'anic law and faith in its Sunni form.

The return to the Sunni tradition of Islam had been launched by Salah al-Din (Saladin), the Kurdish general in the service of the last Fatimid sovereign on whose death he assumed power, founding the Ayyubid dynasty (1171). Under Salah al-Din, the two neighboring cities of Misr and al-Qahira merged to form a single fortified capital, the symbol of a determined military policy to defend Islam threatened by the Crusades. As a great power, Egypt found itself at the center of religious struggles that opposed the Eastern and Western worlds.

Then came the Mamluks, the slave-warriors of Slav origin who were recruited by the Ayyubids to combat the Mongol pressure in Syria; they later overthrew their Arab rulers and took their turn in the splendid residence in the Citadel (1250). Despite their humble origins, these former mercenaries brought two centuries of unsurpassed artistic and architectural splendor to Egypt. Cairo was then a city of dazzling beauty, a true "navel of the world" that the Arab historian Ibn Khaldun (1332–1406) described as "a metropolis of the world, the garden of the universe, a meeting point of nations, a seething mass of peoples, the greatest Islamic center, a seat of power."

Today, many of the Mamluk monuments are among the most elegant in the city. The mosque of Sultan Hassan on the slopes of the Citadel is one of the masterpieces of Arab architecture. Like many of the ancient mosques in Cairo, it was originally a *madrasa*, a theological school that taught the Qur'an. This was the

origin of the magnificent mosques-cum-mausoleums of Qalawun and al-Ghuri, which flank one of Cairo's most famous sites: Khan al-Khalili, one of the largest souks in the Middle East. This maze of alleys, markets, shops, and ancient caravanserais came into being during the Mamluk era in an area where the Fatimid caliphs had their tombs. It brings together the largest variety of people and goods imaginable in a medley of voices and colors made even more picturesque by the unfamiliar tourists who wander around curiously, clutching their souvenirs.

The layout of Cairo was not greatly altered under the Ottoman domination (1517–1789), with the exception of buildings inspired by Turkish architecture. The centuries of subjection to the sultans of Constantinople were ended when independence was regained under the Muhammad Ali Pasha at the start of the nineteenth century, although by this time domination of Egypt was being contested by various European powers.

Under European influence, particularly British and French, Cairo enjoyed a new burst of construction that produced new districts in unmista*ka*ble colonial style that had a strong impact on the layout of the city. Once the city had expanded outside of the medieval walls, it quickly reached down to the banks of the Nile, onto the islands of Gezira (where the tower that symbolizes modern Cairo stands) and Roda (where the Manyal Palace is surrounded by gardens) to cover all of the strip between the right bank of the river and the edge of the desert.

The new districts were graceful residential areas with wide avenues lined with gardens and elegant villas, many of which have since been pulled down to make way for concrete apartment blocks that often show signs of cracking before being finished. Neglect may slowly be destroying the villas of "European" Cairo but some of the districts still maintain their old-fashioned appeal, like Garden City on the right bank, Dokki on the left, and Zamalek in the northern part of Gezira island, with its long-established Sporting Club. The rest of the city, however, has developed in a disordered assembly of modern clusters that reach out into the anonymous suburbs.

The unstoppable demographic rise has led, particularly in the last fifty years, to a vast urban explosion with the creation of immense working-class quarters in underdeveloped areas of the city, for example on abandoned land that lay alongside the old Fustat to the south, on the rocky hill of Muqattam to the east, and in the desert area that surrounds the suburb of Heliopolis to the northeast. Heliopolis is the satellite city created in 1905 by the Belgian Baron Empain that is also known as Misr al-Gadida, "New Cairo."

More recent than Heliopolis, the pleasant residential suburb of Ma'adi about ten kilometers to the south of Cairo has now become an integral part of the capital. Unfortunately, the healthy air of the ancient thermal spa town nearby, Helwan, has been

replaced by the fumes of its heavy industry. Here on the slopes of the Arabian mountain chain there are now only steel and cement factories, but in ancient times fine Tura limestone was quarried to be used in the construction of funerary monuments for the pharaohs and important dignitaries. From the air, the ancient tomb-like quarries carved out of the surface of the rocky plateau are still visible.

Despite being stripped bare of their facing stone for use in the Islamic buildings of Cairo, the astounding size of the pyramids of Giza still makes them a dramatic sight. The plateau of Giza is now under siege from the expansion of Cairo and, seen from the sky, it seems no more than an addendum to the city. Yet the great Fourth Dynasty pyramids that have become the symbol of the pharaonic era have resisted many more than Napoleon's famous "forty centuries." Recent studies have provided a reliable method for working out the date that the pyramids of Khufu, Khafre, and Menkaure were built. The method is based on the reconstruction of astronomical calculations that allowed the ancients to identify the celestial North Pole and therefore to align their monuments more or less correctly. Give or take a little, the pyramids have been dated to the twenty-fifth century BCE.

In addition to the pyramids of the three pharaohs and the much smaller ones of their queens, the area is also the site of a huge burial ground for members of their families, high dignitaries, and priests who, from the Fourth Dynasty until the end of the Old Kingdom, enjoyed the privilege of being buried in the shadow of the tombs of their kings and therefore being protected for all of eternity.

A view from the air reveals the structural unity of the various funerary complexes, which were laid out in accordance with a precise and functional architectural logic for reasons of religion and worship. Aligned northeast to southwest in order of chronology and decreasing size, the huge pyramids are only the culminating point of larger funerary complexes that each include a series of connected buildings used for worship of the *ka* (spirit) of the pharaoh: these were an mortuary temple, a processional causeway, and a valley temple that faced onto a canal of the Nile.

Every artistic expression in ancient Egypt was charged with symbolic and religious meanings that transcended aesthetics and turned the work into a message. In the pyramid-shaped solid that was also a royal tomb, the three-dimensional realization of the pharaoh's omnipotence was simultaneously the translation in stone of the place of the "First Time," that is, the primordial hill from which life originated, or the petrified rays of the sun that embraced the pharaoh-Horus who became Osiris after his death and was transported to the stars of the heavenly vault.

At least five oblong trenches have been found at the foot of Khufu's pyramid each containing a boat. Their purpose is not clear, but they are part of a much more ancient tradition, as is borne out by the discovery of fourteen boats buried in the royal necropolis at Abydos, which in all probability date from the start of the First Dynasty. One of Khufu's barks is forty meters long and perfectly conserved; it has been rebuilt and is now exhibited in a specially built museum on the site of the discovery.

The tomb of the mother of Khufu, Hetepheres, was found between the causeway and the northernmost of the three small pyramids of Khufu's consorts. Her superb grave goods, complete with furniture, form one of the most prized collections in the Egyptian Museum in Cairo.

The great mastaba of Khufu's brilliant architect, Hemiunu, lies among several others in the western section of the necropolis situated the west of the pyramid complex. Hemiunu was the first architect to succeed in producing a pyramid of perfect proportions and unsurpassed size after generations of attempts.

Part of the funerary complex of Khafre—whose pyramid is the only one to have conserved its limestone facing on the tip—was the majestic sphinx that lies on the slope of the plateau next to Khafre's valley temple, which also has a sanctuary in front of it. Cut from a rocky outcrop that rose out of the sand, the image of the pharaoh transfigured into a sun god stares out toward the eastern horizon where each day the rising sun confirms the regeneration of the world. Many times restored and cleared of sand in ancient times (documented by the commemorative stele placed between its paws by Thutmose IV), the sphinx was unable to withstand the military exercises of the Turks, whose gunfire broke off its beard and nose, kept today in the British Museum.

The long band of structures that stretch to the west of the pyramid—and that can only be truly appreciated from above—are thought to have been either lodgings for the workers or storehouses. Like its two larger neighbors, the smallest of the three pyramids, the tomb of Menkaure, was raided in antiquity. The exterior pink granite and limestone facing was removed during the Middle Ages when the monuments had become the equivalent of a quarry, its high quality stone already cut and ready for use. Its valley temple was found to contain sculptural masterpieces of the Fourth Dynasty like the magnificent triads in schist showing Menkaure with Hathor and representations of the nomes (provinces) of Egypt. The area to the south of the causeway includes a series of structures where the construction materials were worked.

Flying over the area to the northwest of the temple, one sees the remains of the tomb of Queen Khentkaus, the mother of the two succeeding kings of the Fifth Dynasty. Rather than a traditional pyramid, the queen preferred a gigantic stone sarcophagus that stands on a platform. Next to it are the remains of the extensive accommodation used by those whose duty it was to continue her posthumous cult. Her consort, the last pharaoh of the Fourth

Dynasty, Shepseskaf, was buried at Saqqara in a similar tomb, thereby demonstrating his wish to be distinguished from his predecessors. His example, however, was not continued.

Flying south along the edges of the plateau of the Libyan Desert, one comes to an area strewn with ruins and partially assembled stone blocks that originally formed the uncompleted pyramid of Zawyet al-Aryan (Third–Fourth Dynasties) and, a few kilometers farther south, the famous sun temple of Niuserra at Abu Ghurab. This new type of sanctuary, dedicated to the worship of the sun, was created during the Fifth Dynasty at Heliopolis, the city sacred to the sun god Ra, whose sons these pharaohs claimed to be. The ruins of the temple are sufficient to give an understanding of the architectural model which, generally speaking, is based on that of the pyramidal complexes, with a valley temple and bark for access to the river, a causeway to connect the valley and mortuary temples, and a large courtyard in front of the mortuary temple in which a colossal obelisk stood in representation of the sun's rays.

All of the Heliopolitan pharaohs except the first and last (who were buried at Saqqara) chose to build their pyramids at nearby Abu Sir, one kilometer south of Abu Ghurab. The aerial view of these complexes is fascinating because above the sand, all that remains of this splendid ancient site lies in complete solitude, without any human presence—so ubiquitous at Giza—to disturb the peace.

After a zone of sand dunes, a few kilometers farther south lies the largest necropolis in ancient Egypt, Saqqara. For more than 3000 years, this site was uninterruptedly worked, providing tombs for kings, nobles, dignitaries, and priests, as well as temples and catacombs for sacred animals. The evolution of funerary architecture from the First Dynasty until the Roman era is recorded at Saqqara, and with it the extraordinary vitality of religious thought that was the force behind and end result of every change.

The royal tombs belong almost exclusively to the Old Kingdom, when the administrative and political capital of Egypt was the nearby city of Memphis. The rulers of the previous epoch—who lived at Thinis and had been buried at Abydos—left only cenotaphs here, which are clearly visible from the air on the northeast face of the plateau, together with the long series of unbaked-brick mastabas of members of the royal families and their notables.

Not far away to the west lie the large underground cemeteries dedicated to sacred animals. From above, only the entrances dug out of the rock and the remains of the chapels in front can be seen. As a manifestation of divine essence, animals were also objects of cult worship and were provided with catacombs for their eternal rest. An incalculable number of falcons, cows, ibises, and baboons were buried in the section farthest to the east near the tomb of Nectanebo II (the last king of Egyptian blood in ancient history) and the temple of Isis, the "Mother of Apis." As one heads into the desert, one passes a group of mastabas from the Old Kingdom, and then comes to the impressive underground galleries of the Serapeum. This was a cemetery dedicated to the Apis bulls, whose cult was closely linked to that of the Memphite god Ptah; the cemetery contains the monumental sarcophaguses of a large number of Apis bulls, dating from the reign of Amenhotep III until the end of the Roman period.

The necropolis in the north section of Saqqara is spread around the oldest pyramidal complex in Egyptian history. The funerary monument that king Djoser (Third Dynasty) wished to create was in accordance with new aesthetic and ideological canons that formed a complete break with the past. The stepped pyramid marks the first step toward a "heavenly" concept of an afterlife among the Eternal Stars for the pharaoh, and was the first representation of the divine status of the pharaoh in stone.

The design, traditionally attributed to the famous architect Imhotep, was centered on the eternal abode of the Lord of the Two Lands being set in a context that perpetuated the aspects most closely associated with his earthly power and that reflected his dual human and divine nature. On the east and south sides of the pyramid there were buildings for the celebration of the sed festival, the royal jubilee in which the pharaoh reaffirmed his physical strength and his dominion over all of Egypt. This nucleus was surrounded by a high enclosure wall with niches and pilasters like the façades of a royal palace. The complex was, therefore, a stone replica of the palace with annexes made from wood, matting, and unbaked brick that Djoser could enjoy after his death.

To the southeast, outside the enclosure wall, the remains of a similar complex that was never finished can still be seen. This was intended for Sekhemkhet, Djoser's successor, whose sarcophagus was found in place but empty.

Between the two enclosures stands the pyramid of Unas, the last king of the Fifth Dynasty, with its superb processional causeway paved with white limestone still partially conserved. The interest of this monument lies in the earliest example of "Pyramid Texts"; these are the oldest body of magical-cum-religious formulas, which were inscribed on the walls of the burial chamber and destined to accompany the deceased into the Afterlife.

The pyramids of the founders of the Fifth and Sixth Dynasties, Userkaf and Teti respectively, stand to the northeast of the stepped pyramid. In accordance with tradition, a large cemetery of splendidly decorated mastabas belonging to functionaries of the epoch lies nearby. Although the Pyramid Texts were the exclusive prerogative of the kings, commoners made use of other forms of expression to aid them in their journey after death. The walls of the funerary chapels bear lively representations of all aspects of the deceased's earthly existence, including work and private life, which were then transferred symbolically into the dimension

beyond the tomb using a series of ad hoc formulas such as the traditional formula of the "reversion of the offerings," which was carved over the entrance and in the inner chapel of the mastaba with the deceased's title and name. This was an effective way to demonstrate to what extent the pharaoh conceded to his subjects the means for a happy afterlife. With the intercession of Osiris or Anubis, the pharaoh provided funerary offerings for the *ka* of the deceased that were magically renewed each time the formula was read. The subject of the pictures or texts was thus activated simply by reciting the funerary formulas.

The private necropolises of the New Kingdom were concentrated in two areas; those southeast of Teti's pyramid are all hypogean tombs dug out of the cliff on which the Bubasteion temple was built in the Late Period for worship of the cat goddess Bastet. The tombs are mostly from the second half of the Eighteenth Dynasty and the Ramessid period and were discovered filled with mummified cats consecrated to the goddess. Many important individuals had been buried here including Aper-El, the vizier of Amenhotep III, who lived at the start of the Amarna Period and whose extraordinary set of grave goods was found almost completely intact. The wet-nurse of Tutankhamun, Maya, was buried a few meters away.

The tombs of a number of equally important figures were found in a second nucleus to the south of Unas's causeway. These were not rock-cut tombs but were built with an external chapel topped by a pyramidion. Examples of this type include the tomb of Tutankhamun's treasurer, also named Maya, and the army general Horemheb who, before becoming pharaoh, had prepared his own tomb here. His royal tomb lies in the Valley of the Kings.

Approaching the southern sector of Saqqara, one comes to a number of funerary complexes that include those of Pepi I, Merenre, and Pepi II (Sixth Dynasty), which all bear fascinating versions of the Pyramid Texts in their burial chambers. More interesting is the fact that these are also reproduced in the pyramids of Pepi II's queens, who were buried next to the king; this fact demonstrates the cautious passage of the pharaoh's funerary prerogatives to members of his family, a privilege that was later extended to commoners with the creation of the Sarcophagus Texts.

In the cultivated area at the foot of the plateau opposite Saqqara stood ancient Memphis, the city that, according to Herodotus, had been founded by Menes, the mythical uniter of predynastic Egypt. The site that today is a sad mass of ruins was once the splendid capital of the Two Lands throughout the Old Kingdom and did not suffer decline until the end of the first millennium BCE, after Alexander's conquest of Egypt. Little or nothing remains of its monuments, of Apries' magnificent palace, or of its many temples, just stones and isolated statues among fields and palm groves. Only fragments remain of the large temple of Ptah, which was once one of the largest religious centers in Egypt and is now partly swallowed up by the modern village of Mit Rahina. The temple's name—*Hikuptah*—was transformed by the Greeks into *Aigyptos*, from which the name "Egypt" is derived.

After the political upheaval that disrupted the country during the First Intermediate Period, the capital was moved to Thebes by the local kings of the Eleventh Dynasty, giving rise to the period known as the Middle Kingdom when it took power. Thebes' political supremacy during this period was, however, short-lived because Amenemhat I, the founder of the Twelfth Dynasty, chose to settle farther north when he built a new residence named Itj-tawy. The ancient location of the city is still unknown but it is logical to suppose that it stood near his main necropolis, Lisht, to the south of Dahshur. Lisht today is no more than a barren desert of ruins dominated by two crumbling hills that at one time were the pyramids of Amenemhat I and his son Sesostris I.

Dahshur, on the other hand, provides a spectacular lesson in the history of architecture. Among the "classic" profiles of pyramids from the Twelfth and Thirteenth Dynasties on the site, there are two of major importance for their shape and their historical value. They are the two funerary monuments built by Snefru, the father of Khufu, in an attempt to transform the structure of the stepped pyramid built by Djoser into a geometrically solid and perfect form.

The first of the two to be built was the one to the south, referred to as the "bent" pyramid because the architects were obliged to alter the slope of the outer walls during construction and thus create a monument with sides at two different angles to the ground. This solution was obviously unsatisfactory to their royal patron who decided to try again, this time avoiding too extreme a slope, and consequently producing a slightly flattened pyramid that, from the color of the stone, is known as the "red" pyramid.

At Meidum to the south of Lisht, the structure sometimes referred to as the "false pyramid" was built earlier; it was finished by Snefru but was probably begun by his predecessor, Huni, the last pharaoh of the Third Dynasty. The structure was also based on a graduated design formed using a new technique of building an outer lining of limestone around a central body. The final stage of construction was to fill in the steps so that the pyramid appeared to have smooth sides. The structural fragility of the pyramid, which was modified several times during construction, resulted in early and serious damage, and now the monument appears to be simply a colossal stone tower surrounded by sand and rubble. Even though Snefru's works were not an architectural success from the viewpoint of formal purity, they pointed the way to the masterpiece created at Giza by Khufu, who inherited from his father not just a kingdom but also the tools for creating one of the Seven Wonders of the Ancient World.

88-89 The island of Gezira is a dash of green in the heart of Cairo. To the north is the residential district of Zamalek; to the south the Sporting Club, various museums, and the Cairo Tower.

91 top Al-Tahrir Square
on the right bank of the
Nile, where the Egyptian
Museum and some of the
most important hotels in
the city are located.

91 center The imposing
neoclassical building that
is home to the Egyptian
Museum in Cairo was
designed by the French
architect M. Dourgnon at
the end of the nineteenth
century.

90 The junction of Abd
al-Monim Riyad Square,
behind the Egyptian
Museum. The Sixth of
October bridge joins the
right bank to the island
of Gezira and the left
bank.

91 bottom The American
University in Cairo
is one of the busiest
cultural centers in the
capital.
It has a library
and a well-stocked
bookstore.

92 top Manyal Palace was built by Muhammad Ali Pasha in the center of a tropical garden at the northern end of Roda Island.

92 bottom The ancient nilometer in Cairo is situated at the southern end of Roda Island. It was built in 715 by Caliph Suleiman to measure the levels of the annual floodwater and to aid in predicting crop growth.

92-93 Monasterli Palace stands at the southern tip of Roda Island. It is an eclectic complex of buildings built at the start of the last century.

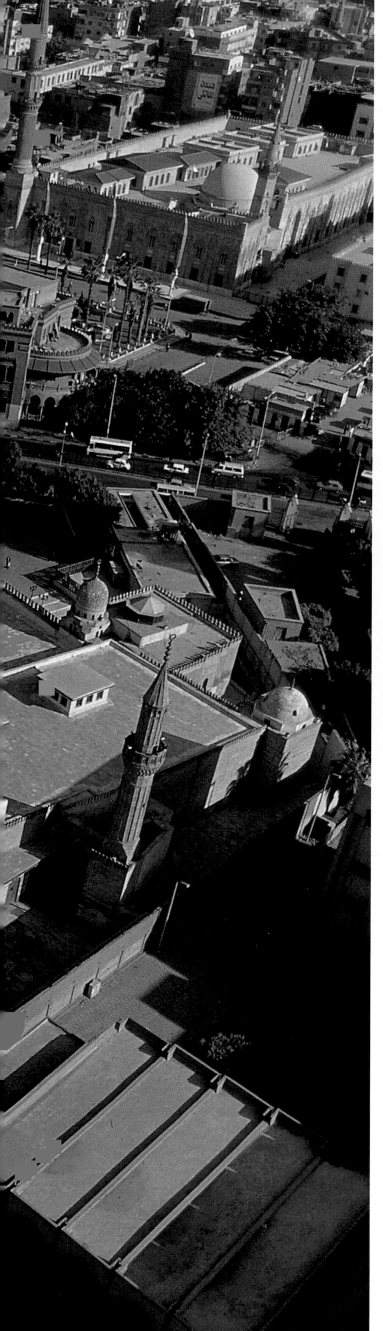

94-95 Al-Azhar mosque, founded in 970 as a study center of Qur'anic doctrine and law, is one of the world's oldest universities.

95 The Fatimid mosque of al-Hakim was completed in 1010. In its eventful existence it has been used as a prison by the Crusaders, as a stable by Saladin, and as a storehouse by Napoleon.

96 The mosque/madrasa (Qur'anic school) of Sultan Hassan (top, with the open courtyard) is a masterpiece of medieval Mamluk architecture. The building next to it is the early twentieth-century mosque of al-Rifai.

96-97 The Citadel dominates the east of the city from a spur of the Muqattam hills. It was built by Saladin in the twelfth century and became the residence of the rulers of Egypt for 700 years. The mosque/mausoleum of Muhammad Ali stands at the center.

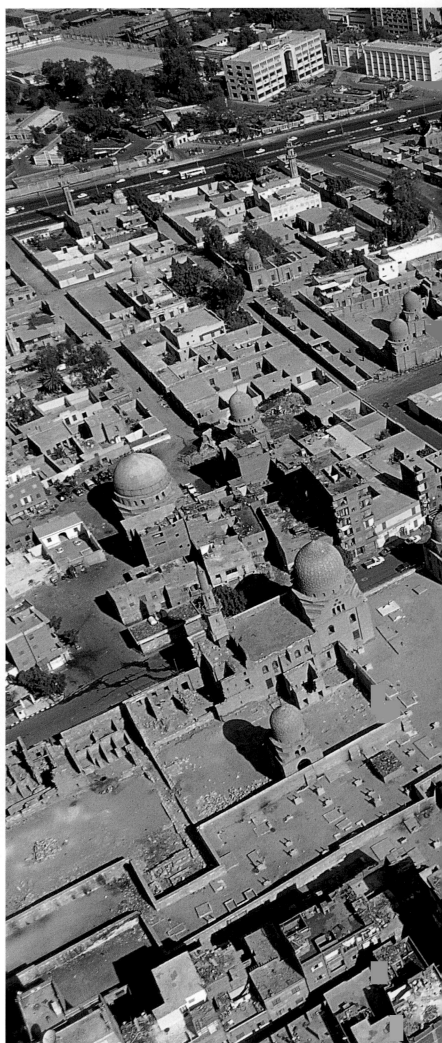

98 and 98-99
The immense City of the
Dead was originally the
cemetery of the caliphs
and the Mamluks but
today is inhabited by
some of the poorest and
most marginalized
families in Cairo.

100 In front of the Mena
House Oberoi Hotel in
Giza, the plateau of the
pyramids and
necropolises of the Old
Kingdom appear like a
mirage rising from the
sand.

101 Almost besieged by
the sprawl of the city, the
symbols of the pharaonic
civilization—the
Pyramids—rise against
the horizon,
imperturbable,
grandiose, and immortal.

*102 top and 103
The sheath of limestone
from the nearby quarries
of Tura remains on the
tip of Khafre's pyramid
showing the original
cleanness of the lines.*

*102 bottom The shadow
of Khafre's pyramid in
the early morning.
Though smaller than
Khufu's, it seems taller
because it was built on
higher ground.*

*104-105 The Giza
plateau with the three
Fourth Dynasty pyramids
belonging to Menkaure,
Khafre, and Khufu (from
left to right).*

106-107 *The body of the Sphinx was carved out of a single out-crop of rock that rose out of the sand. The nose and beard were knocked off by Ottoman soldiers who used the statue for target practice.*

107 top *The Sphinx was recently restored to arrest the advanced state of degradation of the rock. Environmental pollution is a serious threat to the monument.*

107 bottom *The Temple of the Sphinx, in front of the creature's paws, and Khafre's valley temple, with the remains of the processional causeway that leads to the mortuary temple and pyramid.*

108 top Mortuary
complexes belonging to
the rulers of the Fifth
Dynasty at Abu Sir
between Giza and
Saqqara. Niuserra's
pyramid in the
foreground was built
near a solar temple.

108 bottom Little
remains of ancient
Memphis, the capital of
Egypt during the Old
Kingdom. The lovely
alabaster sphinx
probably flanked
the entrance
to the temple of Ptah.

108-109 Djoser's
Step Pyramid
at Saqqara, designed
by the famous
architect Imhotep.
This was the first
attempt to translate
a pyramidal shape
into stone.

110 The "red" pyramid of Snefru at Dahshur. The monument, built by the founder of the Fourth Dynasty, was cased with blocks of reddish limestone.

111 top Snefru's two pyramids at Dahshur; in the foreground the slightly flattened "red" pyramid and behind, the "bent" pyramid. Together they represent the intermediate phases in the construction of a true pyramid.

111 bottom The necropolis at Dahshur at the edge of the desert. The remains of the brick pyramid of Amenemhat III, the last ruler of the Twelfth Dynasty, can be seen on the right.

112 Much of the bent pyramid at Dahshur still has its original Tura limestone facing. In the sections where it no longer exists, it is possible to see the technique used to lay the internal blocks.

113 top The tip of Snefru's double-gradient or "bent" pyramid. The inclination of the upper half was reduced during construction to give the monument greater stability.

113 bottom The "bent" pyramid at Dahshur and, to the south, the remains of the satellite pyramid. The mortuary temple on the east side is a small building with an offering table.

114 The pyramid of Meidum was built during the transition period between the Third and Fourth Dynasties. It was an early attempt to create a solid and perfect pyramid by filling spaces between steps. What remains of the pyramid today is a tall stepped tower that emerges from a pile of rubble. The limestone facing was stripped during the New Kingdom.

115 The pyramid of Sesostris II at al-Lahun. It was built from brick over a frame of radiating limestone blocks that rested on a central body constructed mostly of limestone. The remains of the ancient village where the workers who built the mortuary complex lived were discovered to the northeast.

116-117 The earliest
Coptic monastery
was built in the fourth
century CE in the
mountains of the
Eastern Desert
for the community
of St. Anthony.

117 top The dramatic
wadi that separates
the high plateau of
Galala South
(to the left) from Jebel
Gharib. The rocky
landscape stretches to
the Gulf of Suez.

117 bottom St. Paul's
monastery stands at the
bottom of a wadi, from
where it is possible to see
Jebel Musa (Mount Moses)
in Sinai. The fortified
structure stands over a
church and protected the
monks from raids.

118-119 The entrance to the Suez Canal in the Red Sea at Port Tawfiq. The canal that connects Egypt's two seas was opened in 1869.

119 top The Bitter Lakes were already used by the pharaohs of the Twenty-sixth Dynasty as a means of communication between the Mediterranean and the Red Sea.

119 bottom At 163 kilometers long, the Suez Canal is able to let seventy-five ships pass per day, but it is not wide enough to allow two-way traffic.

Luxor and the Temples of the South

Luxor is a pleasant town on the Nile in the shadow of the Theban mountains, the sacred Mount of the West that keeps watch over the eternal abodes of the great kings of the past and the nobles who served them. Luxor is an obligatory stop for visitors from all over the world who are increasingly drawn to the incomparable archaeological treasures of what was the most magnificent capital during Egypt's most splendid period: Thebes.

The modern city amply reflects the impact of the growing pressure of tourism; the new buildings suffocate the old white-plastered houses protected by gardens of hibiscus and tamarind plants, large hotels have replaced the attractive grand hotels of the early twentieth century, but the Winter Palace Hotel and here and there an elegant villa remind the visitor of what Luxor was like for the first great archaeologists, treasure hunters, eccentric travelers, adventurers, and the cultured European elite enamoured of antiquities. Today the atmosphere is very different. The banks of the river are filled with cruise boats constantly going to and fro between Luxor and Aswan and there is a permanent crowd of trinket sellers besieging anyone who has the faintest appearance of being a tourist. Cafés and small restaurants offer succor to the tired visitor between the picturesque bazaars and shops that cater to western tastes with exotic souvenirs.

Not even the bustling holiday atmosphere that pervades the streets of the town center succeeds in erasing the feeling that Luxor is organized around the "shop and run" sort of tourism that has recently been irreversibly changing the look and feel of pharaonic Egypt, but there is nowhere else in the Nile Valley where myth and history merge in a natural landscape to create a setting of equal drama and beauty.

Outside the urban area, the ruins of ancient Thebes are spread along the river banks like an open museum. They lie among fields of wheat and groves of date palms, here lapped by the sands of the desert, there immersed in the rocky belly of the Libyan mountain chain. Lying opposite one another on either side of the Nile, the city of the living and the city of the dead are two complementary and interdependent worlds, the eastern and western horizons of light and darkness in which the immanence of existence and its transcendence merge and are translated into immortal monuments.

Already legendary at the time of Homer, the extraordinary treasures of the "hundred-gated Thebes" were described in the *Iliad*. This, the most magnificent of ancient Egypt's cities, stood on the east bank occupying the area between the temples of Luxor and Karnak. To the Egyptians, Thebes was Waset, "the Powerful," the mythical place where the hill of alluvial soil stood, on which life was born; it was the land of the god Amun, whose name "the Hidden One" enclosed all the mystery of his origins. He was the "Bull of his Mother," in other words, he was self-generated, and could assume human or animal form (for example, a ram or white goose) when he hatched from the egg he himself had shaped.

The seat of Upper Egypt's provincial government from the time of the Sixth Dynasty, Waset was chosen as capital of the whole country for the first time in the Eleventh Dynasty when the break-up of political power that followed the decline of Memphite authority at the end of the Old Kingdom resulted in the Theban king Nebhetepra Mentuhotep asserting his supremacy over his rivals in Herakleopolis and the reestablishment of the union of the Two Lands under a single crown.

His funerary complex in the lee of the rock amphitheater of Deir al-Bahari on the west bank is a magnificent example of a reworking of traditional royal tombs from the time of the Old Kingdom. It was created as a single complex of tomb, mortuary temple, and valley temple with tree-lined courts, terraces, porticoed colonnades, and hypostyle rooms that heralded the "syringe" form of royal tomb of the New Kingdom dug inside the mountain and culminating in the burial chamber and royal sarcophagus.

When the kings of the Twelfth Dynasty moved the royal residence to Lisht, Thebes kept its role as religious capital of the country, which had been institutionalized by the building of the temple of Amun at Karnak (the nucleus of this temple dated back to the reign of Sesostris I) but the development of monumental Thebes began with the return of the political capital to the sacred city at the start of the New Kingdom following a century of occupation of the country by the Hyksos invaders. The war of liberation and reunification of the kingdom had been the work of the Theban kings who founded the Eighteenth Dynasty and guided Egypt on the path toward creating a huge empire.

This was the age of great military campaigns in Asia and Nubia which were translated into trade and cultural exchanges with the countries around the Mediterranean rim and deeper in Africa. Tributes and wealth flowed to Thebes from all parts of the empire, allowing the construction of prestigious monuments, of which the temples of Luxor and Karnak on the east bank and the funerary buildings on the west bank are still the most prominent symbols.

More than a temple inside an enclosure, Karnak is a series of sacred buildings that occupied more and more space as the centuries passed. Situated north of the city, pharaonic Egypt's most magnificent temple complex is a history book written in stone. It was never finished as each ruler from the Middle Kingdom until the Roman era would add a pylon, a court, a colossus, an obelisk, a stele, etc. Only the view from above gives a full understanding of the layout of the majestic sacred complex. It was dedicated to the Theban triad of Amun (often assimilated to Ra), his consort Mut, and their son Khonsu.

To the north of Karnak's walls lie the ruins of the temple of Montu, the ancient warrior god of the Thebaid, and of Maat, the goddess of justice and cosmic order. To the south, a processional way lined with rams'-head sphinxes leads to the temple of Mut, which lies among palms and shrubs beside its ancient sacred pool. Inside the enclosure of Amun-Ra, a double line of pylons and courtyards built during various eras running north–south and east–west mark the monumental access to the temple proper in which the innermost sanctuary held the god's sacred bark.

120 Tne dawn light illuminates the monumental pylons of the mortuary temple of Ramesses III at Medinet Habu on the west bank of the Nile at Luxor.

121

The emphasis on Amun in the temple of Karnak assumes universal proportions to sublimate not only the creative power of the "father of all things" but above all, his function as guardian deity of the pharaoh. The abode of the "king of the gods" thus became the propaganda center of the king's earthly and divine power and every inscription or representation celebrates the greatness of Amun transformed into a defence of royal power.

In support of this refined theology, a series of sacred festivals was celebrated on a cyclical basis with heavy public involvement. Of these, the most spectacular statement of the divine origin of the Lord of the Two Lands was the Festival of Opet. Every year in the second month of the Flood season (Opet), the simulacra of the Theban triad left the shrines of Karnak on their sacred barks to be carried in solemn procession to the temple of Luxor, Amun's "southern harem." In the innermost section of the temple, far from the gaze of the public, the mystical fusion of the king and his father Amun occurred, in which the pharaoh was transfigured into the image of the god, thus ritually confirming the validity of his ascension to the throne and his exercising of power.

The decoration of the temple, which stands between the river bank and the town center, represents the various phases of the Festival of Opet, the ideological foundations of which find their mythical justification in the divine birth of the pharaoh. This is described in extremely poetic language in the most secret part of the temple, while on the outside walls of the processional colonnade that joins the two peristyle courts the scenes of the river procession, with statues of the king and the gods accompanied by music, song, priests, and the faithful, are a superb record of the sequential details of the ceremonial route.

The twin glories of Amun and Thebes are closely bound just as the temples of Luxor and Karnak cannot be disassociated from the celebration of royal authority. The most logical consequence was the concentration of political power and economic privileges in the hands of the powerful Theban clergy, whose support of the throne was rewarded with gifts of property and fiscal benefits.

This was certainly one of the reasons that prompted Amenhotep IV/Akhenaten to free himself from the influence of the priests in Thebes to found a new capital in Tell al-Amarna. It was a short-lived but revolutionary episode characterized by the turning away from traditional gods, Amun first and foremost, whose effigies were chiseled off the temples of all Egypt. For a decade, the universal god was Aten, the sun disk and visible manifestation of Ra, of whom the pharaoh was the earthly incarnation.

The restoration of the religion of his forefathers by Tutankhamun changed the political balances of the country once more and although the rulers from that time on preferred to live in the north—at Memphis and later Pi-Ramesses—Thebes and its god maintained their roles as institutional guarantors of the continuity of the crown until the end of the New Kingdom.

In the immense Theban necropolis on the left bank of the Nile, the scepter of Amun is shared by Osiris, the king of the world beyond the tomb, the mummy-like god who represents all the dead. As far as the western horizon, the bare valleys in the Red Land intersect and thread through the mountain range, creating a dramatic landscape, a monument to eternity modeled in the earth's crust by the hand of the primordial gods. Here, among the baking, tawny ridges, stands Jebel al-Qurna, the pyramid-shaped sacred mountain that dominates the necropolis. To the north lie the Valley of the Kings and one of its offshoots, the silent Western Valley, where the tombs of Amenhotep III and Ay (Tutankhamun's successor) were dug. For five centuries, from the Eighteenth to the Twentieth Dynasties, the pharaohs were buried in this setting known as the "House of Truth," with the entrances to their tombs concealed by boulders.

It was the need to preserve the royal remains and their magnificent grave goods from tomb robbers, who had broken into the pyramids of the Old and Middle Kingdoms, that forced the Theban kings to hide their tombs by separating the place of worship from the place of burial, with the latter hidden inside the mountain itself. What was lost in monumentality, however, was largely made up for in the magnificence of the layout and interior decoration. Dug deep into the rock, the long corridors connected several rooms that were adorned with a profusion of funerary texts and scenes of the Afterlife on the walls in accordance with the various stages of the ritual ceremonies that accompanied the sovereign on his trip beyond the tomb. The last room, the burial chamber with the sarcophagus, was the symbol of the final stage. It was the place of regeneration, the place in which the sun god Ra merged with the king–Osiris at the end of the nighttime journey through the Underworld. Then the new day was born, and the complementary link of life with death was demonstrated with the merging of the two gods in the "One united together."

Every precaution taken to protect the tombs was, however, in vain. Even by the time the Romans entered the ancient burial places and scratched their names on the walls, the tombs had been raided, the mummies stripped of their jewelry, and the magnificent grave goods robbed. Of the sixty-two royal hypogean tombs found so far, only one avoided being broken into, the tomb of the boy king Tutankhamun. His birth and death are shadowy episodes in the history of Egypt, but his divine face, shaped in the gold of the funerary mask, has survived millennia to the modern day. The mask and the other priceless treasures discovered in the tomb are now displayed in the Egyptian Museum in Cairo.

Smaller but no less beautiful, the rock tombs of the pharaohs' consorts and the princes and princesses who died young lie in the ravines of the small Valley of the Queens to the southwest of the mountain. Many of the tombs were unfinished, others spoiled, but those that time has preserved are decorated with brightly colored scenes, rather conventional in composition but highly stylized in the iconography of the figures, the divine and royal attributes, clothes, and jewelry. These

scenes were integrated with extensive texts from the Book of the Dead, a collection of formulas and spells that were considered essential for the deceased to overcome the dangers in the Afterlife. All these elements are present in the most complex and extensive decorative program, in the tomb of Nefertari, the favorite wife of Ramesses II. Recently saved by restoration from imminent destruction, the tomb is a masterpiece of aesthetic delicacy that the superb execution has made into one of the jewels of the Ramessid period.

Remains of the funerary temples built to accommodate the posthumous cult of the king stand on the southern slopes of the Theban mountain, where the Libyan mountain chain gives way to cultivated land. Despite the west bank being the dominion of Osiris, the intimate relationship of Amun and the pharaoh is overwhelming in these temples. These were the "castles of millions of years," built as temples dedicated to Amun, of whom every sovereign was the incarnation and, in that capacity, the object of worship after death. The temples of the Twenty-eighth Dynasty are mostly just ruins, but the only one to have survived, the "holy of holies" of Queen Hatshepsut, is a superb example of funerary architecture transformed into a political statement. Built next to the temple constructed 500 years earlier by Nebhetepra Mentuhotep in the natural amphitheater of Deir al-Bahari, the airy structure of courtyards and porticoed terraces was designed to be a divine legitimization of the Crown. The famous architect Serenmut created a magnificent and unique building for the "Lord" of the Two Lands that was to celebrate not just the main events of Hatshepsut's reign (like the famous expedition to the land of Punt), but also the queen's divine status. As the daughter of Thutmose I and the widow of Thutmose II, Hatshepsut later usurped the throne from her stepson, the future Thutmose III, who became king on her death. To justify her seizure of power, Hatshepsut called on her fathers: the divine one, Amun, who is shown inseminating the queen (Hatshepsut's mother) with the sacred sperm that would lead to the birth of Hatshepsut herself, and her natural father, Thutmose I, who presents her to the people as his legitimate heir.

Art placed at the service of ideology produced glorious monuments, the organization of which is seen more clearly in the better preserved temples of the Nineteenth and Twentieth Dynasties, for example those of Seti I, Ramesses II (the Ramesseum), and the one celebrating Ramesses III at Medinet Habu, a little south of Thebes.

Enclosed by a high wall of unbaked bricks within the sacred complex, the temple proper is surrounded by stores, craftsmen's workshops, administrative offices, and even a small palace for pharaohs to stay in during official ceremonies like the distribution of rewards for military valor or the celebration of sacred festivals. One of the more important of these was the Festival of the Valley, in which the statues of the Theban triad crossed the Nile in procession to visit the "houses of Amun' (the funerary temples) on the west bank.

The temple of Ramesses III still stands imposingly at Medinet Habu, incorporating a temple dedicated to Amun during the Eleventh Dynasty in its outer wall, and later rebuilt and enlarged by Hatshepsut and Thutmose III. The architecture and the decoration of Ramesses' temple are largely based on the model offered by the Ramesseum, especially in the profusion of scenes celebrating the pharaoh's military victories, which contend for space with the paintings that are more religious in nature. What is original about the complex is to be seen in the structure of the south gate, which was designed to be a triumphal entrance between a series of crenelated towers reminiscent of eastern architecture. They are based on the Syrian *migdol*, a fortified citadel that can be seen in the siege scenes inside the temple.

Behind the funerary temples, the rocky outcrops of the desert are the site of tombs of high functionaries and dignitaries who lived in Thebes from the end of the Old Kingdom to the Graeco-Roman period. The most splendid examples were built during the New Kingdom and reflect the wealth and sophistication of the Theban court at its height.

Unlike those of the rulers, the tomb and the place of worship belonging to private individuals were assimilated to form a single unit that might be entirely or partially dug out of the rock. More rarely, particularly during the Late Period, the external structure was given the appearance of a magnificent temple-palace built above the burial chambers.

The interior decoration of private tombs of the Eighteenth Dynasty was often based on the traditional themes of everyday life, which, to judge by the many scenes depicting banquets, dancing, music, hunting, and abundant harvests, must have been very enjoyable. Each tomb was later personalized with scenes of the most important episodes of the owner's biography—the taking of an Asiatic fort, the collection of tributes from foreign countries, giving archery lessons to the heir to the throne, being awarded royal honors. All the scenes were rendered realistically and in a wealth of detail. Profane scenes were accompanied by religious or funerary motifs such as the pilgrimage to the great temple of Osiris in the sacred city of Abydos, making offerings to the gods, the preparation of the funeral rites, and the funeral procession to the tomb; themes such as these were to become predominant from the Nineteenth Dynasty onwards. Beyond the celebrations of an individual's life and the artistic and documentary value of the paintings in the Theban tombs, the universe represented displays a love of life in all its forms rather than a fear of death. The fear was not denied, but faced up to and dealt with in advance by means of a series of formulas and rituals whose purpose was to ensure the deceased a happy life in the next world.

In the southwest corner of the necropolis, a clearer voice calls out from the past: this is the village of Deir al-Medina, which was founded at the start of the Eighteenth Dynasty to house the workers and craftsmen whose job it was to build the royal tombs.

The need to maintain the secrecy of the location of the royal tombs meant that it was necessary to isolate the workers from the rest of the world. This was done by confining them to a narrow valley in the

heart of the Theban mountains not far from the site of the tombs. The excellent state of preservation of the village shows, in an aerial photograph, the typically orthogonal layout inside the small but comfortable houses aligned along a central axis and enclosed by an unbaked brick rectangular wall. Until the end of the Twentieth Dynasty, generations of highly skilled painters, engravers, architects, and carpenters and their families brought life to this tiny settlement in the desert of the dead, handing down from father to son the sought-after position of "servant in the House of Truth."

Their own tombs were excavated in the slopes of the hill terraces that overlook the village to the northeast. Each one was crowned by a small pyramid and fronted by a four-sided courtyard that led into the cult section cut entirely from the rock. The burial chamber, as in all Theban tombs, was entered via a shaft and was decorated in a lively manner with scenes of happy existence in the Afterlife.

The wealth of inscriptions found in the village and the materials found in the necropolis—on occasion complete sets of grave goods—make Deir al-Medina one of the most important archaeological sites, not simply because it is one of the very rare examples in existence of Egyptian civil architecture, but also because it has made it possible to reconstruct the social and professional life of this small enclave of privileged workers: the organization of work, legal disputes, family arguments, and the deep literary culture. An entire world emerges from thousands of years of silence to recount with immediacy the daily events of the small community that for five hundred years created funerary masterpieces for the great pharaohs and queens of the New Kingdom. The abandonment of Deir al-Medina coincided with the fall of the weak Ramessid dynasty, which left Egypt in a state of political instability. The succeeding dynasties were to transfer their residences to the Delta and leave Thebes in the hands of the Great Priests of Amun.

Undermined from the inside by power struggles, the country was unable to withstand the foreign invasions that for a while turned the conquerors into subjects. The black pharaohs who arrived from Nubia reclaiming their right to the throne of Amun (Twenty-fifth Dynasty) were respectful toward ancient traditions and made their contributions to the construction of Karnak and Luxor as faithful rulers. But the Assyrian and then the Persian invasion jointly delivered a heavy blow to Thebes, though it was to enjoy a final moment of glory under the Thirtieth Dynasty and the Ptolemies. However, by the time of the Roman era, Thebes was just another of the many cities of Upper Egypt eclipsed by new ones and destined to survive only on the ruins of its ancient splendor.

Like their indigenous predecessors, the new Greek and Roman rulers also conformed to the models provided by Egypt's past and presented themselves to the people as the legitimate heirs to the throne of the Two Lands. In this context, the construction of temples to local gods and the celebration of important religious festivals had the important role of confirming the continuity of the dynastic succession. It was not by chance that many of the great temples built during this period were constructed on the ruins of more ancient ones, respecting the architectural canons of classical tradition but with particular insistence placed on the cosmogonical function of the monument and on the complex ritual that transfigured the house of the god into the mythical place of the creation of the world.

Several Ptolemaic temples still in good condition were built in the area of Thebes—at Dendera, Esna, Edfu, and Kom Ombo—and their well preserved structures allow us to admire the stately and superb architecture that represents the last bulwark of Egyptian faith before it was swept away. Seen from above, it is possible to recognize the basic architectural similarities of the temples, regardless of their variations in layout, which all interpret the archetypal image of the primordial hill emerging from the waters of primeval chaos.

The distribution of the rooms and the decoration were designed to give material form on the walls, ceilings, and ground to the laws that governed the harmony of the world, the most important being the worship of the gods, who are the guarantors of the world's well-being. The temples are separated from the outside world by a high wall built in wavelike sections that imitate the hostile forces of the muddy ocean that existed before Creation. Inside, the main pylon was decorated with scenes of the king defeating his enemies, symbolizing the victory of order over the disorder that constantly threatened the created world of which the temple was the metaphor.

The profile of the pylon is reminiscent of the hieroglyph for the horizon, which was a symbolic boundary beyond which a universe of symbols and sacred texts existed to recreate the mythical context in which the world came into existence. The writings are evident: the measurements of the temple had to correspond to an ideal model set down by the gods during the "night of time" because it was to serve as the "House of the First Time," that is, the place in which time and space became measurable and life began on earth.

The message is effectively translated into the decorative program of the large hypostyle room that evokes the natural setting of the beginning of time within the eternity of cosmic cycles. The roof is a starry firmament with zodiacs and the celestial gods; the bases of the walls teem with aquatic plants, pools, and animals, above which the forest of columns with plant-like capitals emerges. The fundamental myths of Egyptian culture, of creation, rebirth, and the maintenance of the set order are widely illustrated inside the temples together with liturgical motifs associated with the cult of the god.

As one approaches the innermost areas, the rooms become smaller and the light dims to the point of darkness in the innermost room where the sacred bark and a stone shrine with a statue of the god were placed. A series of chapels and small side chambers surround the "venerable house" and inscriptions and images illustrate the

use of the various rooms the and ritual ceremonies that were held in them: the care of the divine statue taken each day by the priests, bays for storing offerings and furnishings, rooms to prepare balsams and ointments, the treasure room, the library.

Other buildings were annexed to the larger temple, such as the House of Truth, in which sacred texts were copied and studied, the priests' accommodation, and storerooms. The sacred pool was the symbol of the ocean from which the sun appeared at the dawn of Creation and in which the priests and pilgrims purified themselves each day. During the nighttime celebration of the Mysteries, initiates took part in the representation of the death and resurrection of Osiris.

The presence of *mammisi* ("Birth Houses") and the *sanatorium* was typical of Graeco-Roman temples. The first was where the mystery of the divine birth of the king took place, as used to happen in ancient times in the temple of Luxor. The second was used for medical cures made using magical rather than scientific practices, including sleep therapy.

The layout of the sacred complex at Dendera, dedicated to Hathor, is perfectly preserved. Besides the main temple with its columns with extraordinary Hathor capitals (the face of the goddess with the ears and horns of a cow), there are the *mammisi* of the pharaoh Nectanebo and another used by Roman emperors, and the *sanatorium*, with its basins for performing ablutions in the purifying waters, and chambers where patients fell into cataleptic sleep in which Hathor was supposed to reveal the most effective remedy for their complaint. Then there is the pool with steps, a nilometer, a rostrum, and an aviary; today the pool is overgrown with palm trees in a memory of the sacred copses of acacias and sycamores that used to grow in the temple enclosure.

The temple's precious and secret cult apparatus was kept in the twelve magnificently decorated crypts. The equipment was used for celebrating the mystery rites that were prohibited to the profane. The simulacra of the goddess, her attributes, and furnishings made with gold, silver, and electrum appear on the walls with a crowd of deities and symbols linked to the myths of creation and regeneration.

During the Festival of the New Year, the gold statue of Hathor left the crypt and was taken to the small pavilion in the southwest corner of the upper terrace of the temple. Here, at dawn on the first day of each year, the mystical union of the goddess with the sun took place, ritually realizing the mythical event of the first morning of the world, when the sun rent the darkness and life was born from light.

The remains of a similar building have been found in the temple of Horus at Edfu, 100 or so kilometers south of Thebes. This temple is the largest surviving temple from the Ptolemaic period. The original complex occupied a much more extensive area, since buried beneath the fields and buildings of the modern village, and included the same types of buildings as those at Dendera. Once a year the statue of Hathor made the long trip up the Nile to her spouse at Edfu,

where fifteen days of celebrations were held with dancing and music, and the lively participation of the local population.

Horus (the falcon-god) was the dynastic god *par excellence*; he was the posthumous son of Osiris of whom every pharaoh was the incarnation. The legend of Osiris tells that he was the first of the kings to rule the earth but was killed in envy by his brother Seth and cut into pieces. Osiris's spouse, Isis, found the hidden parts of her husband's body, put them back together, and reanimated them with her breath of life so enabling the legitimate heir, Horus, to be conceived. Much of the decoration of the temple tells the story of the struggle between Seth and Horus, which ended with the triumph of good over evil. Horus became the new king of the earth and his father Osiris the lord of the kingdom of the dead. It was therefore at Edfu that the ceremony commemorating the crowning of the king was held, during which a live falcon was taken from the sacred aviary, crowned in the central court, and placed in one of the inner rooms where he "reigned" for a year as the living symbol of Horus.

Another form of Horus was worshiped in the temple at Kom Ombo. This was Haroeris, Horus the Elder, who shared the sanctuary with the crocodile-god Sobek. The dual cult gives the monument a unique architectural structure, which has two sacred rooms and two of each of the gateways and passages that lead to it from the outer pylon. A small chapel dedicated to Hathor from the Roman period just inside the enclosure wall is used today as storage for the mummified sacred crocodiles buried in the nearby necropolis. Standing high over the Nile and surrounded by sand, the ruins of Kom Ombo present a spectacular sight when viewed from the air.

The temple of Khnum at Esna is very different. To the Greeks the ancient town of Esna was Latopolis, where the camel caravans arriving from Sudan would be welcomed. The only part of this temple that has survived is the superb hypostyle hall, which emerges from a hollow 9 meters below the level of the village. Inside, there is a continuous spread of texts and images on the walls and columns that dispenses with the structural function of the architecture, turning it into a mere support for the decorations. Esna provides examples of the last stage of Ptolemaic–Roman hieroglyphic writing, which had by that time become not just a simple language tool but an alchemy of thousands of signs combined in cryptographic inventions that could be deciphered only by initiates. This system was especially effective for the writing of divine names, in which each sign represented the sound and one of the god's many qualities. Thus the name of Khnum—the ram-god who formed humanity on his potter's wheel—appears on twenty-four columns in 140 different ways.

As the era of pagan Egypt approached its end, the country's religious heritage was defended in increasingly obscure forms that were only interpretable by the elected few, and the temple became the sacrosanct representation of a millennia-old metaphysical idea transcribed into the incorruptible stone of the last sons of Horus.

126-127 The Nile at Luxor: on the right bank the city, on the left bank the Valley of the Kings; in the foreground the Jolie Ville Mövenpick Luxor Resort on Crocodile Island.

128-129 The great complex of Karnak temple dedicated to the Theban triad of Amun, Mut, and Khonsu. In ancient times, a processional way, lined with sphinxes, connected the temple to a landing stage on the Nile.

129 The sacred enclosure to the south of the temple of Amun contains the remains, including a pool and small temples, of the complex dedicated to Mut. A long avenue of sphinxes joins the two complexes.

130 The spectacular hypostyle hall in the temple of Karnak. The ceiling was supported by 134 colossal columns erected and decorated during the Eighteenth and Nineteenth Dynasties.

131 top The temples of Ramesses III (right) and Seti II (left) face one another in the court in front of the hypostyle hall; in the center, the surviving columns from Taharqa's kiosk.

131 bottom The hypostyle hall seen from the southern pylons; in the foreground, the courtyard of the Cachette, which contained thousands of statues that originally decorated the temple.

132-133 The magnificent architecture of the sacred complex at Karnak. For more than two thousand years, the "Most Chosen of Sites" was ideologically and economically the most important center of pharaonic Egypt.

134-135 The rising sun grazes the shadows of the Theban mountains; on the opposite bank, the usually busy world around the Temple of Luxor is still drowsy.

136 The processional colonnade of the Temple of Luxor, the "southern harem of Amun." Scenes from the Festival of Opet are shown on the walls surrounding the columns.

137 Inside the entrance pylon, the imposing columns of the Temple of Luxor flank two porticoed courtyards joined by the processional colonnade.

138-139 The Libyan desert is the majestic setting for the royal tombs of the Valley of the Kings. The peak on the left is the sacred mountain that watches over the royal necropolis.

140 A path between
the western valleys
of the Theban
necropolis leads
to the Valley of the
Queens, where the
consorts and children
of the pharaohs
were buried.

141 The village of Deir
al-Medina was built at the
beginning of the New
Kingdom for the
craftsmen and artists
who worked on the royal
tombs; below, the small
Ptolemaic temple of
Hathor.

142 The massive statues of Amenhotep III, called the Colossi of Memnon by the Greeks. It is said that at dawn the sun-warmed stone used to produce a melodious sound that resembled the song of Memnon, the son of Aurora (dawn), in response to the morning greeting of his mother.

143 The colossal statues of Amenhotep III stand majestic and alone on the threshold of where his mortuary temple used to stand. The necropolises of the New Kingdom are in the mountains in the background.

144 The huge rock-hewn amphitheater of Deir al-Bahari with the temples of Nebhetepra Mentuhotep (Eleventh Dynasty) and Queen Hatshepsut (Eighteenth Dynasty).

145 The mortuary temple of Hatshepsut was an elaboration of the acclivitous design of the monument next to it, built in a series of ascending ramps, courts, and porticoed terraces.

146 The heart of the mortuary temple of Ramesses II (the Ramesseum). The porticoed temple with colossal statues of Osiris leads to the hypostyle hall and inner sanctuary.

147 top The mortuary temple of Seti I at Gurna. The first two pylons have disappeared, but the sanctuary dedicated to Amun-Ra and the posthumous cult of the king has superb reliefs.

147 bottom The aerial view of the Ramesseum reveals the unusual alignment of the long sides of the temple; they are parallel, but oblique to the outside walls.

148-149 The mortuary temple of Ramesses III at Medinet Habu. The enclosure wall surrounds a royal palace, storerooms, apartments for the priests, a small temple of Amun, and the tombs of the God's Wives of Amun.

149 top The temple of Ramesses III is based on the plan of the Ramesseum: it has two porticoed courts and three hypostyle halls that lead to the inner sanctuary.

149 bottom The monumental entrance on the south side of Medinet Habu is based on the architectural model of Syrian forts, featuring high, turreted walls fitted with windows.

149

150 In the shadow
of the Libyan mountains,
the ancient tombs
on the plain of Dra Abu
al-Naga share
the area with the
houses of the
modern village.

151 A Muslim funeral
in the village of al-Gurna,
located at the foot
of the rocky slopes
where the tombs
of the high dignitaries
of the Eighteenth
Dynasty lie.

152-153 The thick fronds
of the palms resemble fire-
works exploding in the sky.

154-155 Many villages lie
on the fertile strip of land
that borders the west bank
of the Nile.

156-157 The Nilotic
landscape near Edfu is
ringed by the warm
colors of the desert
mountains, the intense
greens of the fields, and
picturesque farming
villages.

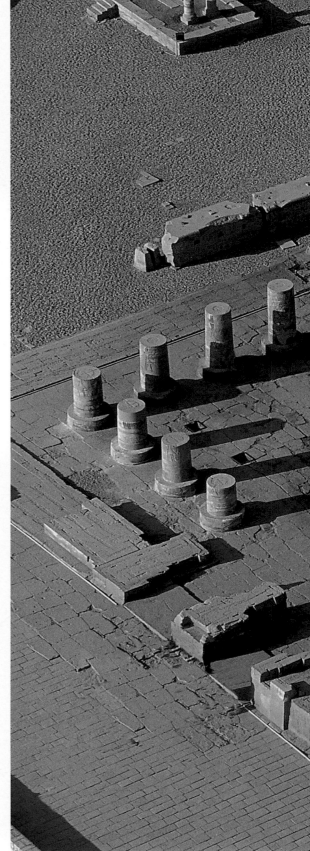

158 top The sanctuary of Hathor at Dendera. From the left, around the great temple lie the temple of the birth of Isis, the sacred pool, the sanatorium, the Ptolemaic mammisi, a Christian basilica, and the Roman mammisi.

158 bottom The temple of Edfu stands among the houses of the modern village. It is one of the best-preserved examples of sacred architecture from the Ptolemaic period.

158-159 The double entrance to the temple of Kom Ombo leads to the dual sanctuaries of Haroeris and Sobek. The oldest section of the complex was built in the First Intermediate Period and later enlarged by the Ptolemies.

160-161 The monumental pylon of the temple of Horus at Edfu is decorated with colossal reliefs of Ptolemy XIII. The portal is flanked by two large granite statues of the falcon god.

162-163 A river cruise between Luxor and Aswan offers lovely views of the villages that stand on the rocky edge of the desert.

159

Aswan and Lake Nasser

Just north of the Tropic of Cancer where the Nile pushes its way through the granite and sandstone blocks of the First Cataract, lies Aswan, the pearl of Upper Egypt. Arriving from the north, the river seems suddenly to spill out from the desert sands, racing between rocks and islands in the wide rocky amphitheater that encloses one of the most enchanting places in the Nile Valley. This is a land in which light and color mingle and heighten one another in natural contrasts of great beauty. The whole scene is dominated by the strong presence of the river, the sky, and the rock walls of the river banks.

The modern city lies on the right bank. The architecture is simple and graceful, with minarets poking above the roofs of the houses and the gardens. The urban landscape is characterized by soft, amber hues reflected by the surrounding dunes onto the buildings. The many colors of man-made and natural products enliven the bazaar stalls and the clear air is pervaded by the smells of the spices and essences that are a long-established part of Aswan's trade. From on high, surrounded by the fronds of palms and gardens, the turquoise water of the swimming pools in the large hotels adds to the palette of colors and removes some of the emphasis on the ocher bands of sandstone reflected in the waters of the Nile.

The development of tourism in Aswan is more contained and less invasive than in other towns and cities in Egypt. It started at the beginning of the nineteenth century, when the appeal of the place and the fashionable interest in Egypt following Napoleon's expedition spread throughout the West. What had been just a small Nubian village was transformed into a pleasant resort where wealthy Europeans came to spend the winter months.

The blue of the river is as pure as that of the night sky, broken here and there by the white sails of the feluccas that carry modern tourists, just as in the past, to the local antiqui-

ties. The pharaonic city and its temples were not built on the banks of the river but on the green island of Elephantine that lies opposite Aswan. A fortress defended naturally by the turbulence of the river, the ancient Swenet was a frontier city and the base for military and commercial expeditions into Black Africa—ancient Nubia—from where caravans loaded with incense, gold, ivory, exotic goods, and convoys of wretched slaves would arrive.

The southern tip of the island is where the archaeological remains are clustered; it includes the ancient residential area, the temple of Khnum (the ram-god who created the world and was worshiped as the lord of the cataract with Satis and Anukis), and a series of sacred buildings from various eras. The most unusual of these is dedicated to Heqa-ib, the Sixth Dynasty prince of Elephantine, who was deified after his death. Like those of other "Guardians of the Door of the South" and dignitaries of the Old and New Kingdoms, his tomb lies in the rock necropolis on the west bank that faces Aswan.

A little farther to the south, a large and vivid green garden that emerges from the river is the lush botanical garden created at the end of the nineteenth century by the British consul Horatio Kitchener. It is an explosion of tropical plants and flowers that give off a blend of powerful exotic perfumes. Beyond the sandy slopes of the western bank opposite, the ancient monastery of St. Simeon, one of the largest in Egypt, was built to accommodate hundreds of monks and pilgrims, but the still solid and well-preserved complex has been abandoned since the fourteenth century.

Working one's way against the current between the rocks and islets covered with flowers and plants, one comes to the small island of Sehel where there are ancient graffiti and inscriptions. One of these, the Ptolemaic "famine" stele, records the name of the builder of the stepped pyramid at Saqqara,

164 The coast of Lake Nasser north of Dakka. The creation of the largest reservoir in the world submerged thousands of square kilometers of land including most of the Nubian homelands.

Djoser-Netjerkhet. Much of the text on the stele refers to the quarrying of the high-quality stone for which the district of Aswan is famous: quartzite, calcite, and, above all, the red and grey granite that was used to construct obelisks, colossi, and monolithic shrines for statues of the gods.

The same hard granite was used at the beginning of the twentieth century to build the first Aswan dam; this was an important step in the exploitation of the power of the Nile, but it was not sufficient. The water-related problems remained pressing and the only possible solution was the construction of a second, much larger dam farther south that resulted in the creation of a huge reservoir, Lake Nasser.

Though the dam has brought undeniable benefits to agriculture and has provided hydro-electricity, it has also produced a drastic alteration in the hydro-geological balance of the area between the first and second Cataracts. The entire region between Aswan and Wadi Halfa, where the river used to run through the rocky landscape, is now submerged by the lake.

If we can still admire splendid temples built by the pharaohs of the "Golden land," it is only thanks to the timely intervention of UNESCO, which mobilized the world to save the most important monuments from the waters. Entire temples were disassembled and reconstructed on higher ground as similar as possible to the original locations. Ten have remained in Egypt, and four have been donated to each of four countries as a thank you for their contributions to the engineering work involved.

The archipelago of islands that lies in the immense rocky amphitheater of the First Cataract at one time included the enchanting Philae, an island enhanced by the purity of the colors still visible in the great temple of Isis. With construction of the first dam, the temple was regularly flooded to the top by the water held back by the barrier, and it was only for three months each year when the water was allowed to flow that the buildings were once more exposed to view. The sight was extraordinary: it gave the site's rare visitors the sensation of being present at the Creation, which according to myth took place inside the temple. When the pylons emerged from the water, the soil sprouted spontaneously with vegetation that was pictorially continued in the decorations at the base of the walls and columns of the temple. The annual emergence of the temple from the waters and the rebirth of plant life seemed a renewal of the primordial marsh from which the organized world materialized. During the 1970s, after the construction of the High Dam, the temple of Isis and other buildings inside the sacred enclosure were transferred to the nearby islet of Agilkia, the banks of which were cut to resemble those of the island of the goddess that had been covered by the river.

Farther south, beyond the High Dam, lies Lake Nasser, the largest reservoir in the world. It is surprising how this man-made feature blends into the natural environment without impairing the natural beauty; on the contrary, it enhances the spectacular harmony of shapes and colors. Seen from the air, the Nubian landscape is transformed into a piece of jewelry with the lake a blue stone set in the gold of the desert below a limpid turquoise sky that imbues the water with the clarity and luminosity of its all-encompassing space. As it must have been during the dawn of the world, the liquid and solid elements embrace one another and unite without merging, creating tongues of sand, flowery banks, lumps of rock, and levels of dunes against the brown background of the highlands. The lake stretches for hundreds of kilometers without any human presence except for the occasional fishing boat or Bedouin camp.

Here and there one can see temples on the banks, temples that would now be submerged beneath the lake if they had not been moved from their ancient sites. Near the High Dam

there stands the small rock sanctuary of Beit al-Wali and the large Ptolemaic temple of Kalabsha dedicated to the Nubian god Mandulis. A short distance away, Hathor's pavilion with its elegant columns is the only monument to have survived from the great complex of Kertassi. Much farther south, near the ancient Sebua, one can still see the golden profiles of the half-rock temple built by Ramesses II for Amun-Ra, with its avenue of crowned sphinxes in front and, on the nearby hill that slopes down into the lake, the pylons and temple of Dakka dedicated to Thoth by the Ptolemies.

The only ancient settlement to have remained in its original location can be seen on the island of Qasr Ibrim, the highest part of a massive sandstone hill that, before construction of the dam, dominated the east bank of the Nile. The site contains the remains of the temple of Taharqa, one of the last Nubian rulers to have governed Egypt during the Twenty-fifth Dynasty, the ruins of a pharaonic fort that was reused by the Arabs, and the ruins of an early Christian church.

The temple of Abu Simbel, the most dramatic symbol of the efforts made to save the Nubian monuments, stands close to the border with Sudan. The two rock temples excavated from the red rock during the reign of Ramesses II now look out over the lake from about forty meters higher than their original level. In just four years, the temples were literally sawn into 1,036 enormous blocks and reassembled on the top of the hill with the external structures set against a mound of reinforced concrete inside which the internal sections of the temple were fixed. The whole was then covered by rocks to disguise its artificial nature and make the site as faithful as possible to the original location.

Only an aerial view gives away the secret of the extraordinary operation; the frontal view extols the magic of the place with its facades protected by colossal stone statues that inspire respect and admiration. Of the seven temples that Ramesses II built in the remote regions of Nubia, those at Abu Simbel are undoubtedly the most impressive. The Great Temple bores more than sixty meters into the mountain and is fronted by four colossal statues of the pharaoh in full majesty with his royal brides, princes, and princesses at his feet. The manifest purpose of the entire complex was the celebration of the glory of an all-powerful ruler, the "Beloved of Amun," who already had himself worshiped as a god during his lifetime.

The inner pronaos is held up by eight Osiris pillars bearing the image of the dead king, designed to glorify his triumphs as a warrior. The elaborate images of the famous battle of Qadesh against the Hittites fills an entire wall with images of sieges, chariots, prisoners of war, and everywhere the victorious pharaoh supported by Amun. Twice a year, the rising sun penetrates the temple entrance to illuminate the three statues of the gods to whom the temple was dedicated: Ptah, Amun-Ra, and Ra-Harakhti. A fourth statue placed between them represents the deified Ramesses.

As proof of his love for his favorite queen, Nefertari, the king had a temple built next to his own expressly for worship of the queen, associated with the goddess Hathor. The royal couple appear on either side of the entrance in six colossal statues that seem to emerge from the rock itself; four are of Ramesses and two of Nefertari as Hathor. Nefertari's temple is smaller than the Great Temple; it has a hypostyle room with eight Hathor pillars decorated with religious scenes, a vestibule, and a temple dedicated to Hathor. The goddess emerges from the back wall as a heavenly cow protecting a statue of the king, who stands in front of her.

The miracle of Abu Simbel has restored to the world one of the most prodigious examples of the genius of the pharaohs, and thanks to those who saved it we can still today experience the same emotions as all who have been spellbound by it over the millennia.

168-169 The enchanting African landscape seen in Aswan—the "pearl of Upper Egypt"—embraces a varied archipelago of wooded, rocky islands, of which Elephantine is the largest.

172 A superb building in Moorish style built right on the river, the Old Cataract Hotel was used as a setting for the film Death on the Nile, based the Agatha Christie detective novel of the same name.

173 top The small paradise on the island of Amun, in the middle of the river, has been turned into a tourist village.

173 bottom The mausoleum of the Aga Khan on the west bank opposite Aswan was built of pink sandstone in the architectural style of the Fatimid tombs of Cairo.

173

174 North of the Old
Dam in Aswan, the
course of the Nile loses
its clearly defined shape
and is diffused into a
multitude of channels
and inlets.

175 St. Simeon's
monastery, on
the left bank of the Nile,
was built in the sixth
century, but was
abandoned some
700 years later.

*176 and 177 Feluccas
plow the placid water of
the Nile between the
luxuriant islets; a few*
*days' trip on one of the
traditional boats is one of
the most popular tourist
activities.*

178 top The temple of Isis seen in the mirror of the Nile. During the 1970s, the temple was transported stone by stone from the island of Philae, today submerged below the water, to the island of Agilkia.

178 bottom The creation of Lake Nasser has transformed the rapids of the First Cataract into a tranquil expanse of water that is a habitat for water flowers.

178-179 The islands that break the surface in Lake Nasser are actually the tips of rocky desert hills that have been mostly covered by water.

180-181 Dakka temple is one of the ten saved by UNESCO before the lake invaded the Nubian desert. It was rebuilt forty kilometers south at al-Sebua. Many pharaohs contributed to the small sanctuary dedicated to Thoth at Dakka; the temple was founded by the Ptolemies and enlarged by the Meroite king Arqamani and later by the Romans.

181 top The two temples of Dakka (background) and Maharraqa (foreground) were rebuilt near al-Sebua on the west bank of Lake Nasser. Maharraqa temple, built during the Roman era, was dedicated to Serapis and Isis but it was never completed. Today only the relics of the hypostyle hall remain.

181 bottom Wadi al-Sebua, the "Valley of the Lions," earned its name from the avenue of sphinxes that leads to the half-rock temple that Ramesses II dedicated to "his Father Amun."

182-183 A great wall of sand winds from the rock hills down to the lake.

184 To the north of Abu
Simbel, the tip of a
mountain pokes through
the surface of Lake
Nasser like an atoll at sea.

185 A small channel
pushes through the plots
of land at the edge of the
desert, bringing life to
the kingdom of sand.

186 The Great Temple of Ramesses II (along with the Small Temple of Nefertari) was completely dismantled and reassembled in an artificial hill above its original location.

187 top The four colossal statues of Ramesses II at the entrance to the Great Temple were cut completely out of the rock; each stands roughly twenty meters high.

187 bottom Thanks to UNESCO, the two rock temples of Ramesses II at Abu Simbel still command the heights while basking in the rays of the god Ra in Lower Nubia.

188 and 189 The dark
rocks of the desert
landscape northwest of
Abu Simbel have been
sculpted into cupolas by
the implacable erosion of
the wind and sand.

190-191 The changing
landscape of Lake Nasser
north of Abu Simbel
looks like a vast
primordial lagoon
flooding into the rocks
of the desert.

The Western Desert and Oases

Squeezed between the two desert ranges that line the course of the river, the Nile Valley seems a miracle of the creative force of nature, like a green-speckled snake. The vegetation crowds the sides of the river along the valley and into the Delta. But outside of the rich and fertile strip of life regulated by the Nile, Egypt is an arid desert, called the "Red Land" by the ancients to distinguish it from the "Black Land" of the valley's silty soil.

Like majestic propylaea, the cliffs of the Arabian and Libyan deserts are the entrances to the silent kingdom of the unknown, the kingdom of everything that was external, extraneous, and hostile to the ancient Egyptians. The deserts were the mysterious universe that marked the limits of the known world, beyond which the sun rose and set each day in an eternal cycle of heavenly and underworld journeys.

Whereas the Eastern Desert is sculpted by its natural boundary, the Red Sea, the Western Desert is still, in many ways, *terra incognita*, which occupies more than two thirds of the entire country. It is an immense expanse of dunes and rock formations of all natures and shapes that forms the eastern edge of the Sahara.

The landscape was very different tens of thousands of years ago, the land offered areas that were favorable to human settlement, depressions created by geological change and supported by a water table and frequent rains. The many oases were rich in water and vegetation, and an abundance of diverse wildlife—as many rock paintings illustrate—populated the surrounding savannah and formed part of the diet of the prehistoric communities. Progressive desertification of the Saharan area forced the inhabitants towards the Nile around 3200 BCE, but the oases were never completely abandoned and were integrated into the pharaonic state as outposts at the gates of the Sea of Sand.

One hundred kilometer southwest of Cairo, the ocher desert encircles the oasis of Fayoum, a vast green swathe bounded to the north by the waters of Birket Qarun, which was known to the Greeks as Lake Moeris. During the age in which Herodotus lived, the Fayoum was already an expanse of vegetable gardens and fields that supplied Egypt with all sorts of natural products, including citrus fruits, walnuts, olives, and sugar cane. The oasis is a natural reserve teeming with aquatic life and lake birds, and the traditional mud-brick houses have changed little over the centuries. To the ancient Egyptians, Fayoum was the "Country of the Lake," a lush island on the shores of the large water basin (which actually filled all of the oasis during the Neolithic period). In fact, it is not really an oasis at all because the lake receives a flow of water from a branch of the Nile, the Bahr Yussuf.

Fayoum has enjoyed two flourishing periods in its history: recognizing the agricultural potential of the region, the pharaohs of the Twelfth Dynasty built their capital at nearby Lisht and began an intensive program of land reclamation in the marshes, which had been used by their predecessors only for hunting and fishing. The level of the water was progressively lowered to claim more cultivatable land from dried terraces. Temples, towns, and necropolises were built. At Hawara, on the southeastern edge of the oasis, Amenemhat III built a second pyramid (the first is at Dahshur) and a superb funerary temple that had twelve courtyards and 1,500 rooms on two floors. It so astonished Herodotus and Strabo that it was known during the classical era as the "Labyrinth."

Later, the Ptolemies transformed Fayoum into one of the richest and most populous provinces in the country, lowering the level of the lake, increasing the arable land, and settling new colonies of former Greek and Macedonian soldiers. Building was undertaken with new vigor as can be seen by the monumental ruins in the oasis. A number of temples were dedicated to Sobek, the guardian deity of the oasis in the form of a crocodile. Built during the Twelfth Dynasty and enlarged and restored on a number of subsequent occasions, his principal temple stood in what is now Medinet al-Fayoum, known by the Greeks as Crocodilopolis and by the Romans as Arsinoe. Pilgrims visited from every

part of Egypt to feed the sacred crocodiles, which were looked after by the priests and embalmed when they died.

Thousands of demotic and Greek papyruses found at many sites in the region, and the famous funerary paintings on wooden panels that covered the faces of the Roman mummies, known as "Fayoum portraits," are evidence of the intellectual vitality and artistic and cultural originality of these communities which were not at all marginalized from the valley civilization.

More isolated but no less "Egyptian" are the five western oases of Siwa, Bahariya, Farafra, Dakhla, and Kharga. They are a world apart, surrounded by the absolute solitude of the Libyan desert, where the silence is practically deafening. They are the last frontiers of the known universe, the links in a natural chain that curves along geological fault lines that run almost parallel to the Nile. From a strategic viewpoint, the oases have played a fundamental role in the defence of the southeastern edges of the kingdom and the commercial routes that connected Nilotic Egypt with the heart of Africa. Pharaohs stationed governors and military garrisons there, political exiles always found safe refuge, and caravan routes crossed the area, bringing goods and contacts from the external world. The wine of the oases was famous, particularly the one from Bahariya, which was even mentioned in the distant Theban tombs. The vines are no longer there, having been replaced by Egypt's best date palms, juicy citrus, and other fruit trees.

Siwa lies in an isolated position, close to Libya in the northwest of Egypt, between the burning dunes of the Great Sand Seaand the Qattara Depression. It is a green island lost in the desert, but it is self-sufficient thanks to its land being watered by over three hundred springs, and thus is politically more autonomous as well. It has closely guarded its cultural identity over the centuries, maintaining its local language, Siwi (a dialect of Berber), and preponderance of Berber traditions and customs intact. It is a magical world, an ocean of palms and fruit trees tinged with the colors of oranges, pomegranates, and dates, which were the pride of the inhabitants even in antiquity. A remarkable, unspoiled landscape lies all around below the clear sky: white limestone outcrops are reflected in the blue water of the large saltwater lakes that millions of years ago were one sea; mountains are honeycombed with tombs and lined with villages that cling to the rocks; and ancient temples hang over the surrounding desert like ghosts. Barricaded among mud houses on Aghurmi citadel to the east of Siwa, the temple of the Oracle of Amun has long ceased announcing prophecies, but the steps to the sacred stones arouse deep emotions—the same, perhaps, as Alexander the Great felt when he came here to pronounce himself pharaoh. The spot dominates the entire oasis and overlooks all the local landmarks: the great temple dedicated to Amun by Nectanebo II (Thirtieth Dynasty) and known as the "Temple of the Sea" because its limestone blocks are marked with marine fossils and shells; "Cleopatra's Bath" farther to the south, where pilgrims purified themselves in its magical waters, which are cool by day and warm at night; the Mountain of the Dead to the northwest; and the ruins of Shali to the west, an ancient mud fortress that was practically "dissolved" by three days of torrential rain in 1926.

The mirage of Siwa is wrapped in marshy vapor as one heads off toward Bahariya oasis, the vineyard of the pharaohs. The golden yellow sand heaped in constantly transforming waves once more becomes sovereign until one reaches the black quartzite stretches that surround Bahariya. Everything is black, the mountains, the canyons, and even the soil that is covered by pitch quartzite of volcanic origin. A Graeco-Roman necropolis recently discovered at Bawiti, where Alexander built a large temple, contained thousands of intact mummies, painted sarcophaguses, and funeral masks lined with gold.

The presence of many thermal springs gives the oasis an extraordinarily luxuriant vegetation and makes the lives of the inhabitants particularly pleasant; so pleasant, in fact, that a khedive had a large holiday palace built on the black hill that overlooks the depression. This too is now a ruin, wrapped in a black mantle like all the ancient monuments of the area.

Farther to the south, the dark veil over the dunes suddenly begins to sparkle with spots of white in the sun. From on high, the desert around Farafra looks as though it could be part of the surface fo the moon, with gypsum formations that the wind has eroded into fantastic shapes; they poke out of the ocher sand creating spectacular color contrasts that change throughout the day. Under the unbelievably starry night sky, the white protuberances seem to float like ectoplasm, petrified spirits called up by the wind that keep guard over the "No Man's Land." Sometimes shiny flowers of black hematite, fossil corals, and shells emerge from the sand.

The immensity of the dunes continues all the way to Dakhla, a huge oasis divided into three distinct sections: the first is rocky and dominated by the picturesque medieval village of Qasr, with its crude brick minaret, its madrasa, and its ceramics shops.

At its feet, the desert is dotted with fortifications, temples (such as Nero's temple recently restored), and rock tombs from the Roman era frescoed with zodiacs and scenes from the afterlife. The second section has many thermal springs, where the cultivated land is vivid green and the colors of the cliff to the north are soft at dawn but flame red at sunset. The fields in the third part of the oasis center around the small modern town of Mut, built on the slopes of a citadel, its clusters of mud-brick houses in a maze of alleyways and scrub perched on the rock. Farther east are the dramatic remains of the settlement that was the seat of the governor of the oasis during the Sixth Dynasty and its monumental necropolis.

The last oasis, Kharga, is the gateway to the Sahara. It lies in a vast depression 200 kilometers long and 30 wide, defended to the north by a series of Roman forts and dotted with temples protected by high walls. The monuments mostly date from the Late and Graeco-Roman periods, but there are some examples of early Christian buildings, abandoned monasteries and Coptic cemeteries, like the one at Bagawat in the gentle dunes north of Hibis that has 263 chapels in Roman-Byzantine style.

The great temple of Hibis is one of the oldest in Kharga; it was begun during the Twenty-sixth Dynasty and completed by Ptolemy II; splendid wall decorations from the reign of Darius I (Twenty-seventh Dynasty) show the entire Egyptian pantheon around Amun and Osiris. It was under Darius that the oasis flourished as an economic and religious center of prime importance among the peripheral areas of Egypt and it maintained this supremacy until the arrival of Islam.

The introduction by the Persians of new irrigation techniques increased the agricultural potential of the land, and the adoption of the camel as a means of transport shortened distances and increased trade.

One hundred kilometers south of al-Kharga lie the ruins of the ancient fortified site of Dush, a frontier town that developed around the temple of Osiris and Isis that stands on the top of the hill. From here one can look out over the "Forty Days Road" that connected the region of Darfur in Sudan with Assiut in the Nile Valley.

Known as a commercial route during pharaonic times, it became notorious when caravans of slaves were marched from Sudan, who, after forty exhausting days, reached the markets of Egypt before being sold on to Arabia. Today Kharga is at the center of the "New Valley" project, a plan to repopulate the western oases through the creation of new agricultural settlements that will help to ease the saturation of the Nile Valley. In the near future, the safe refuges of ancient political fugitives and the last custodians of desert culture will once more welcome exiles from the Nile Valley.

196-197 The salt lakes near Shali in Siwa oasis resemble a lunar landscape.

198 The poignant ruins
of old Siwa, the city built
of mud, with tapered
towers and tall fortified
walls. In the background,
the limestone hills that
frame Lake Siwa.

199 The old fortified
citadel of Shali in the
heart of Siwa. Built on
rock from blocks of salt-
mud, the fort was largely
dissolved by a torrential
rainstorm in 1926.

200 top Like a swimming pool in the middle of the desert, Lake Siwa lies six kilometers from the center of the oasis. It is salt water, but is clean and can be used for swimming.

200 bottom The gold of the desert and the brilliant green of the fields contrast with the pure blue of the sky and emerald-green water of the lake.

200-201 *The white outcrop of Jebel Bayda is reflected in Lake Siwa. In the background, the splendid landscape of rock and sand that surrounds the oasis.*

201 top *A tank for collecting fresh water from the spring. The artesian wells in the oasis often provide thermal water, but only one-third is drinkable.*

202-203 *The salt lakes and lagoons that ring the oasis are a reminder of the vast sea that once covered North Africa tens of millions of years ago.*

204-205 The luxuriant sea of palms at Siwa encloses the remains of the temple dedicated to Amun at the foot of the sanctuary of the famous oracle.

205 top The spectacular remains of the temple of the oracle of Amun among the ruins of the old city; imposing ghosts on the rock of Aghurmi that overlooks the whole oasis.

205 bottom The hill of Shali background with the ruins of the fort dissolved by rain. Rock temples from the Saite and Ptolemaic periods surround the base of the Mountain of the Dead.

206-207 The ruins of the temple of the oracle that consecrated Alexander the Great pharaoh of Egypt and divine son in 331 BCE. The complex was founded in the seventh century BCE by Saite pharaohs.

208-209 The wildness of the Libyan desert reappears just outside Siwa in rocky highlands and deep depressions.

210 top *The Valley of the Golden Mummies at Bahariya. Recent excavation work has unearthed an underground Graeco-Roman necropolis with hundreds of mummies, many of which wore gilded masks.*

210 bottom *Splashes of green among the ocher and black dunes herald the fertile oasis of Bahariya. Dramatic hills blackened by deposits of iron, basalt, and quartzite surround the oasis.*

210-211 *The largest village in the oasis, Bawiti, has around 30,000 inhabitants. Bahariya's main crop is dates.*

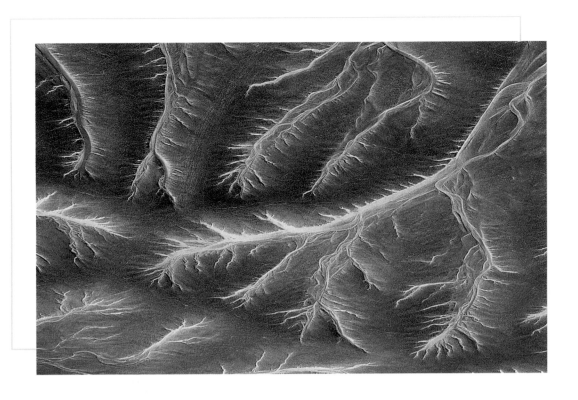

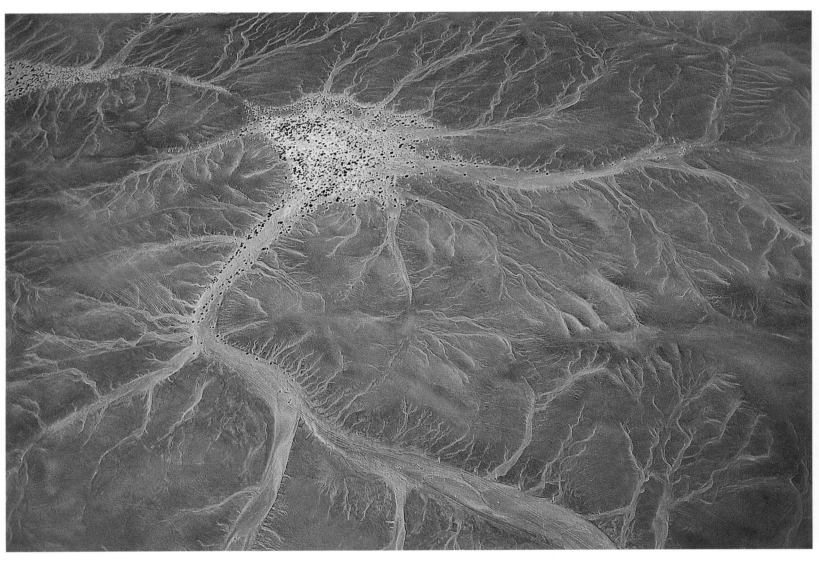

212 The incredible ramifications of the desert wadis to the north of Bahariya form a network that stands out against the surface deposits of black quartzite.

213 The desert landscape furrowed by water courses from antiquity resembles the surface of the moon.

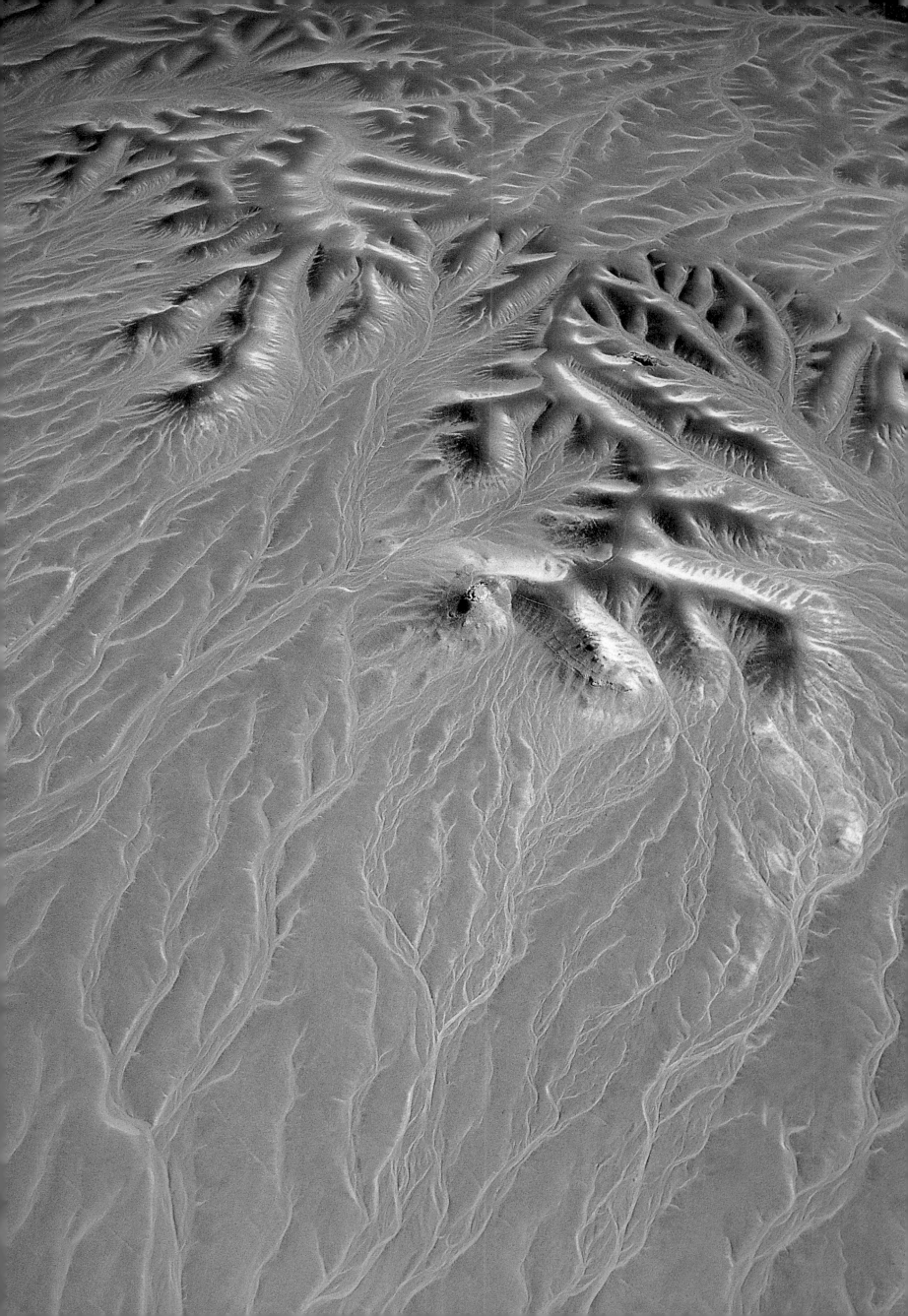

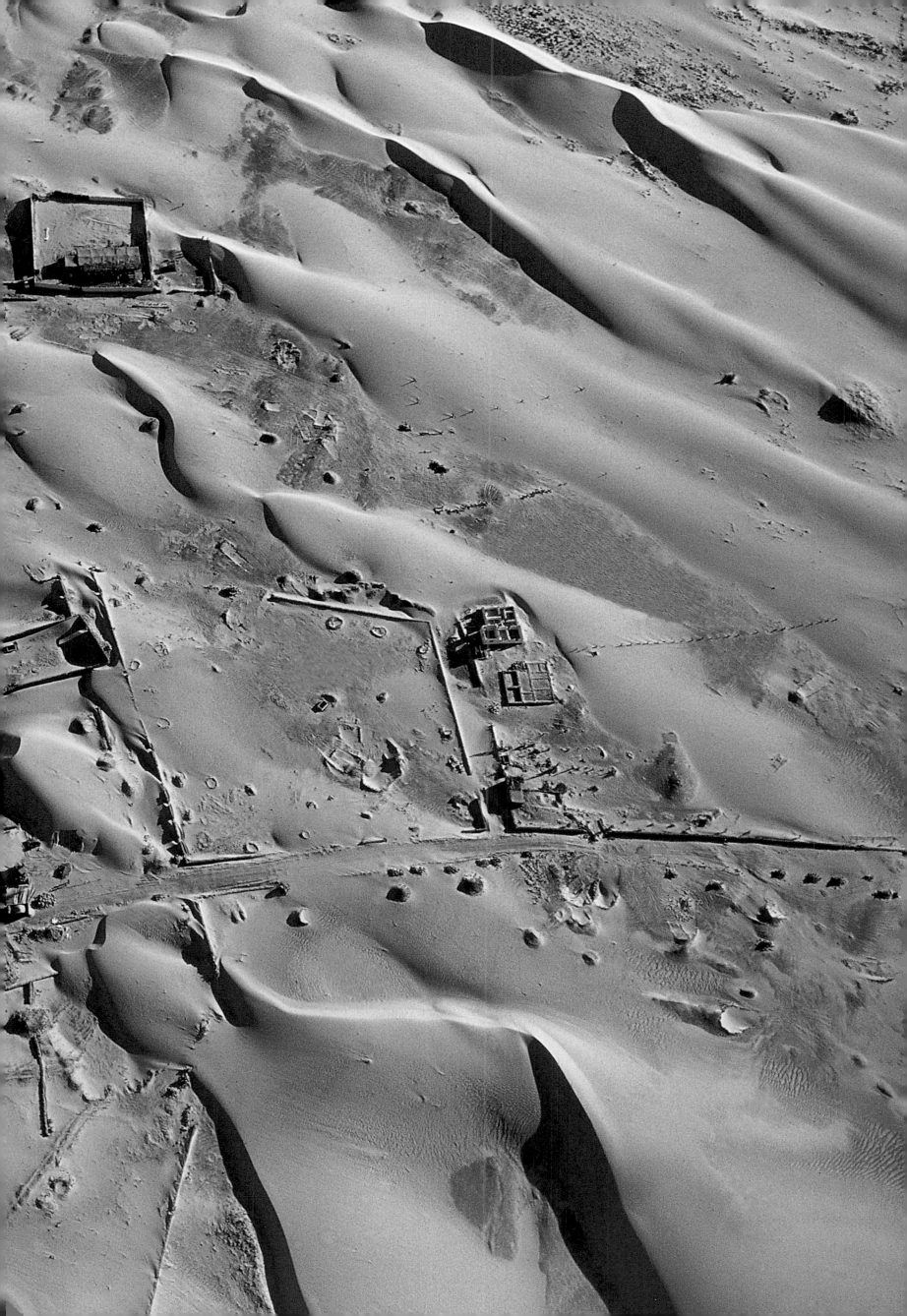

220 and 221 The White
Desert near Farafra lies
on a limestone massif
from the Cretaceous
period, the remains of
which look like milky
spurs.

222 and 223 As it withdrew from this area, the sea left layers of limestone and sandstone, which were then shaped by the wind.

224 and 225 Like flows
of white lava, the
limestone expanses
stream into the sun-
baked sand.

226 and 227 Limestone
formations eroded by the
wind over millions of
years rise from the white
and gold carpet of the
desert. These
extraordinary natural
sculptures have taken
on surreal shapes.

228-229
The metaphorical
landscapes of the White
Desert are transfigured
into atolls lost in the sea
of sand.

230-231 Farafra is the
smallest oasis in the
Western Desert and is
mainly inhabited by
Bedouins. The recent
discovery of sizeable
water reserves has given
a boost to the limited
agricultural resources.

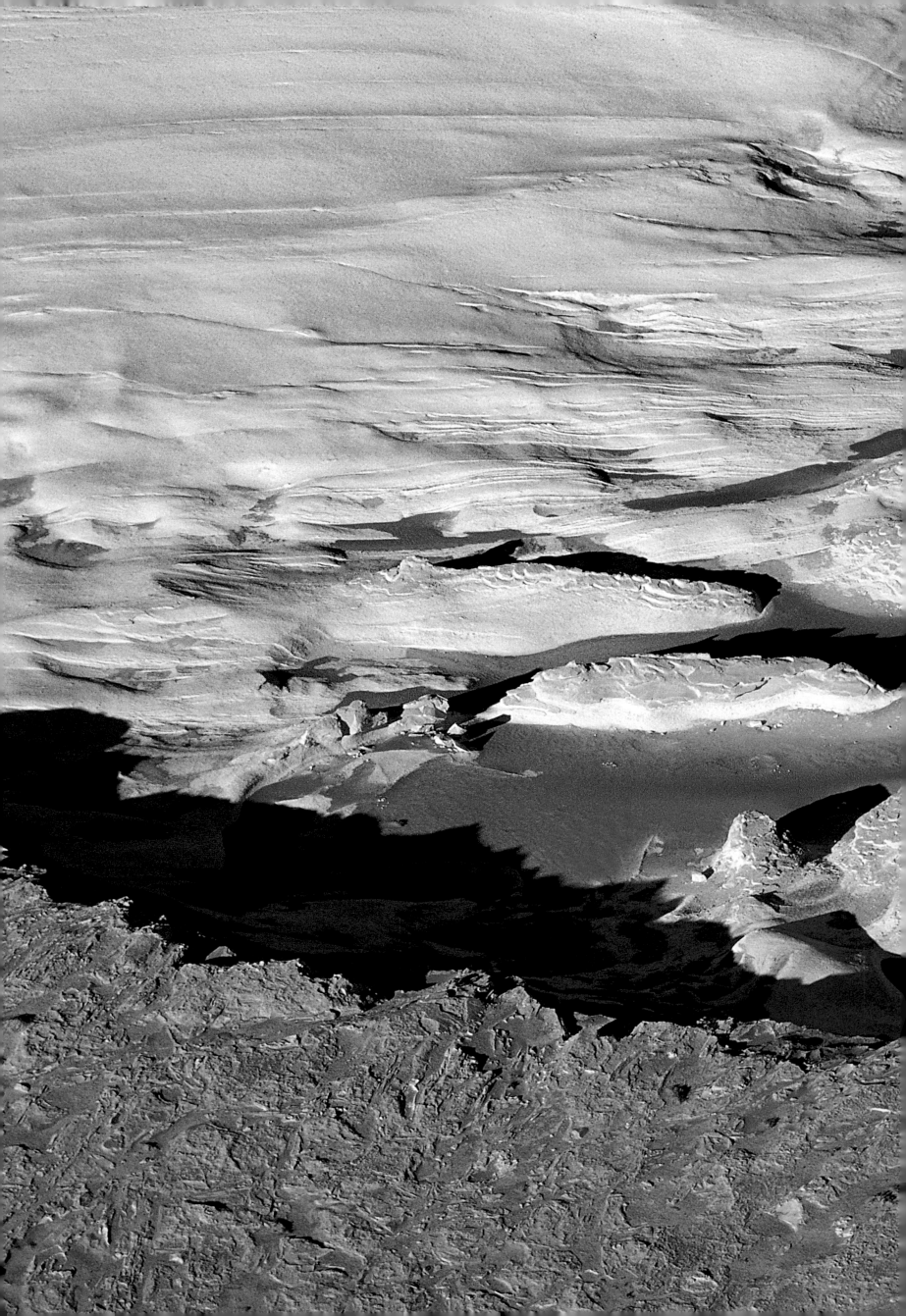

Index

318

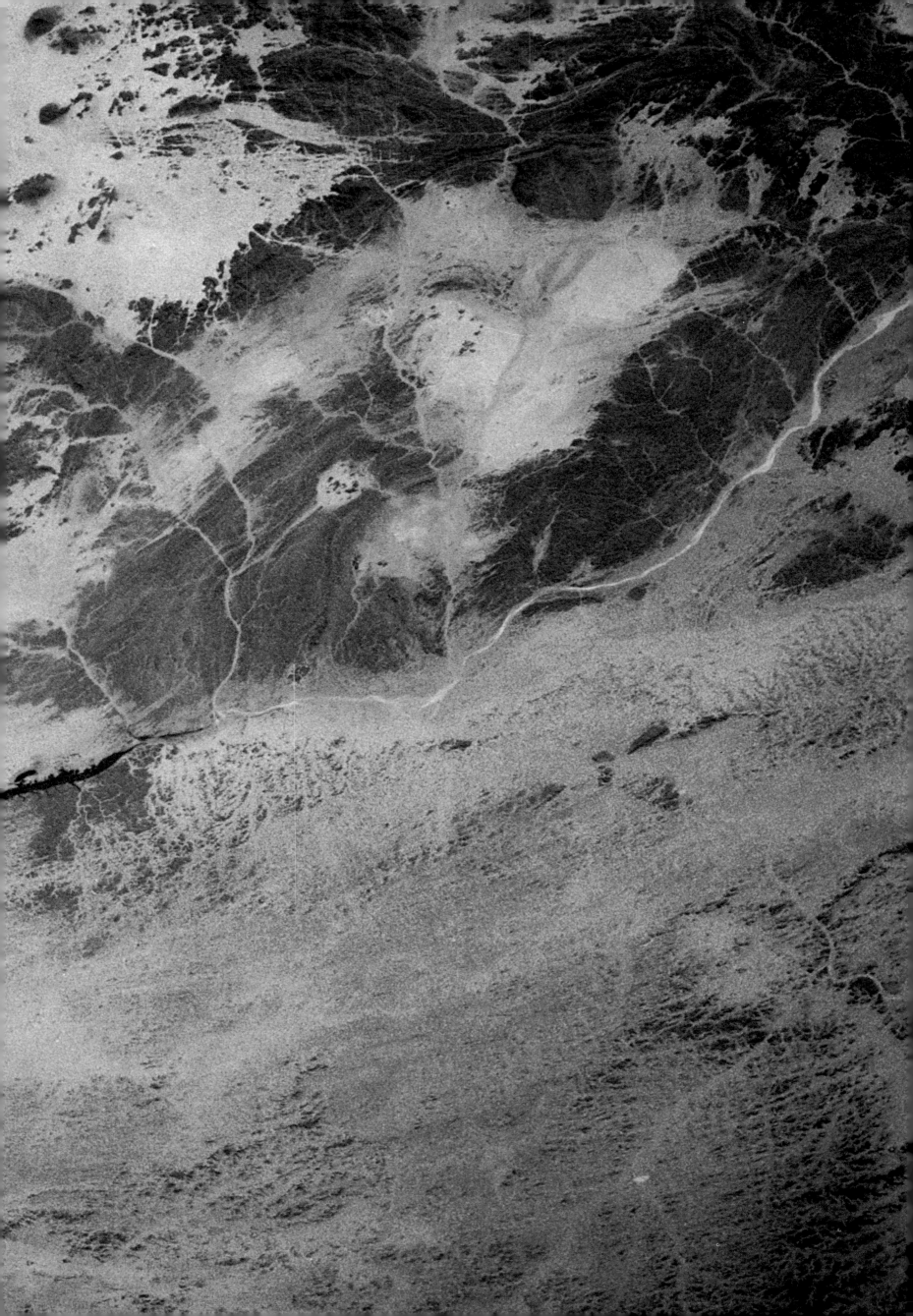

314 With the Aswan High
Dam, Lake Nasser held
back the waters of the
Nile, forming a huge
reservoir that influences
the surrounding
environment.

315 The impressive
course of the Nile, seen
from the southwest.
First through Lake
Nasser and then around
the broad curve of Qena,

its path crosses
the desert. In the
background, the scene
is crowned by the Sinai
Peninsula and the
Red Sea.

316-317 Lake Nasser
(bottom left) with its
branch connecting to Wadi
al-Allaqi. Water, areas
with sparse vegetation,
and the desert sand make
up the tricolored scene.

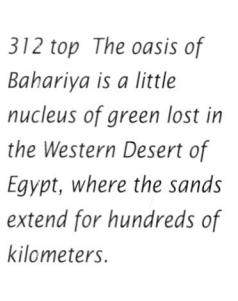

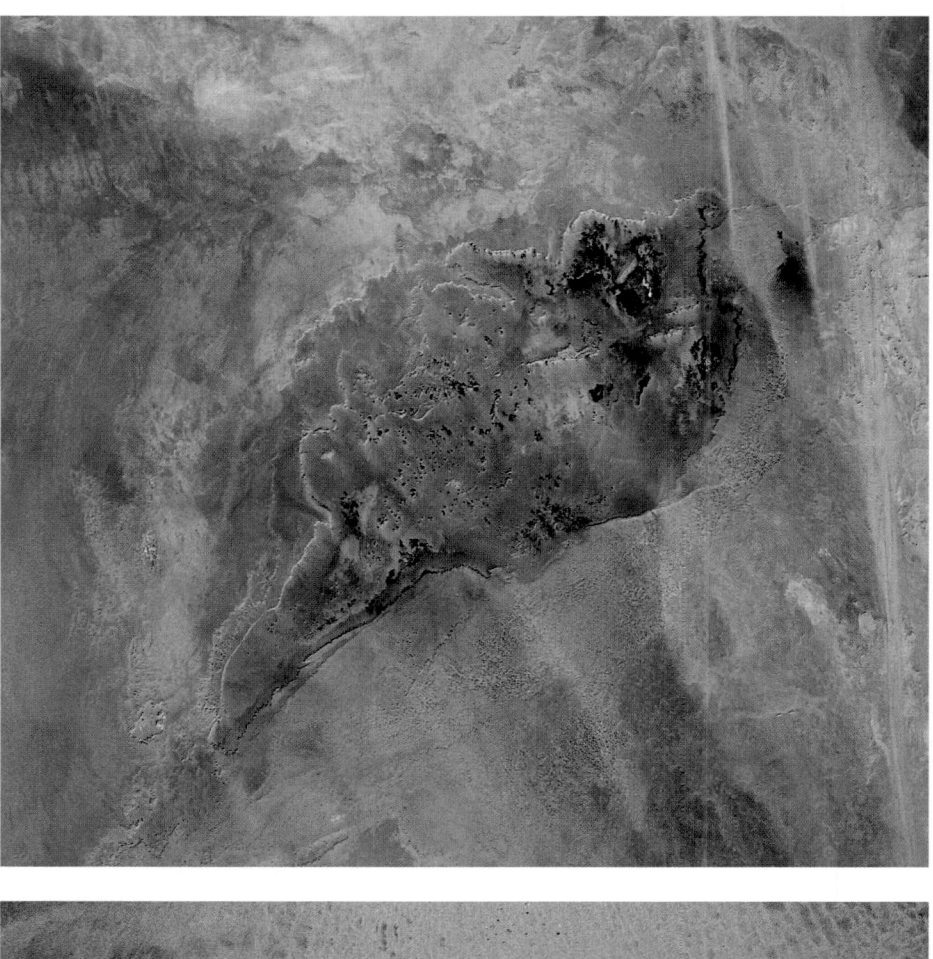

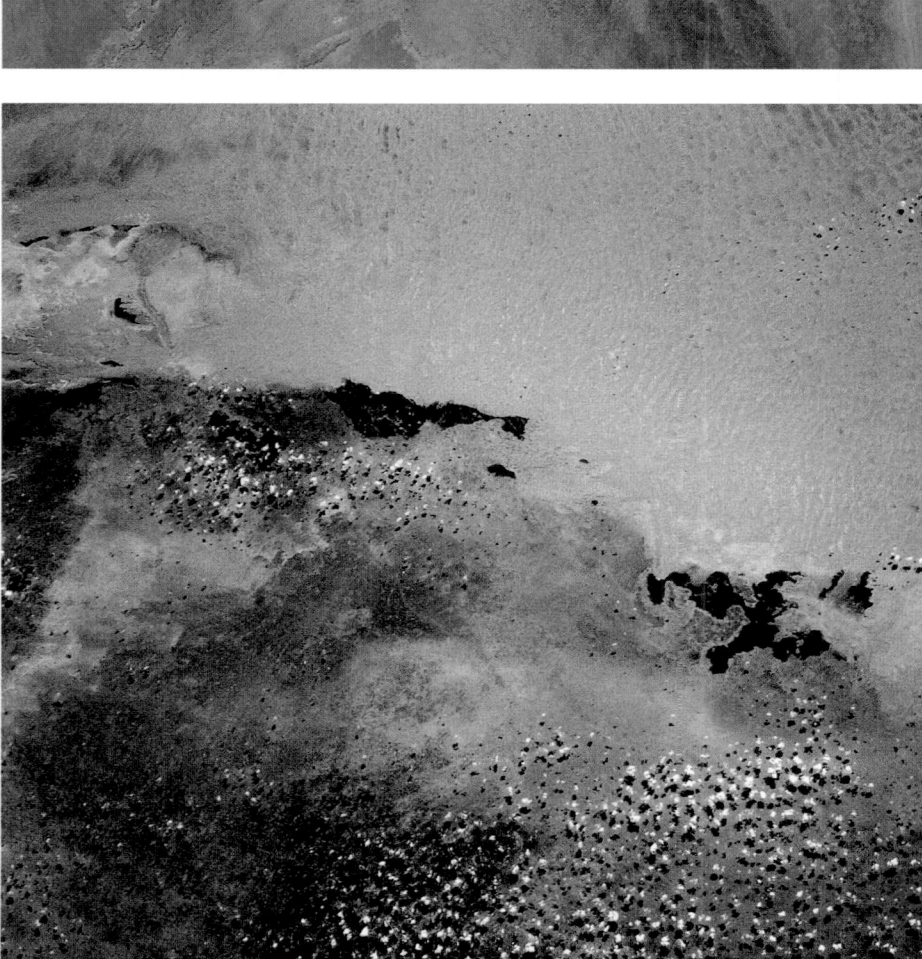

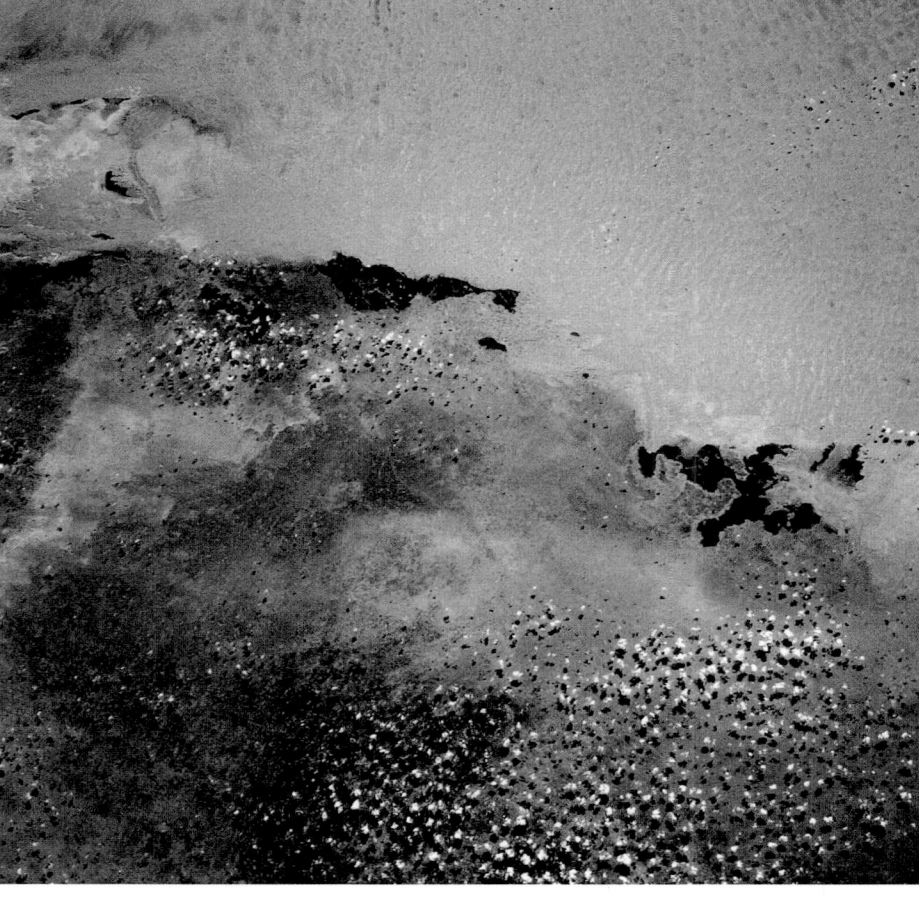

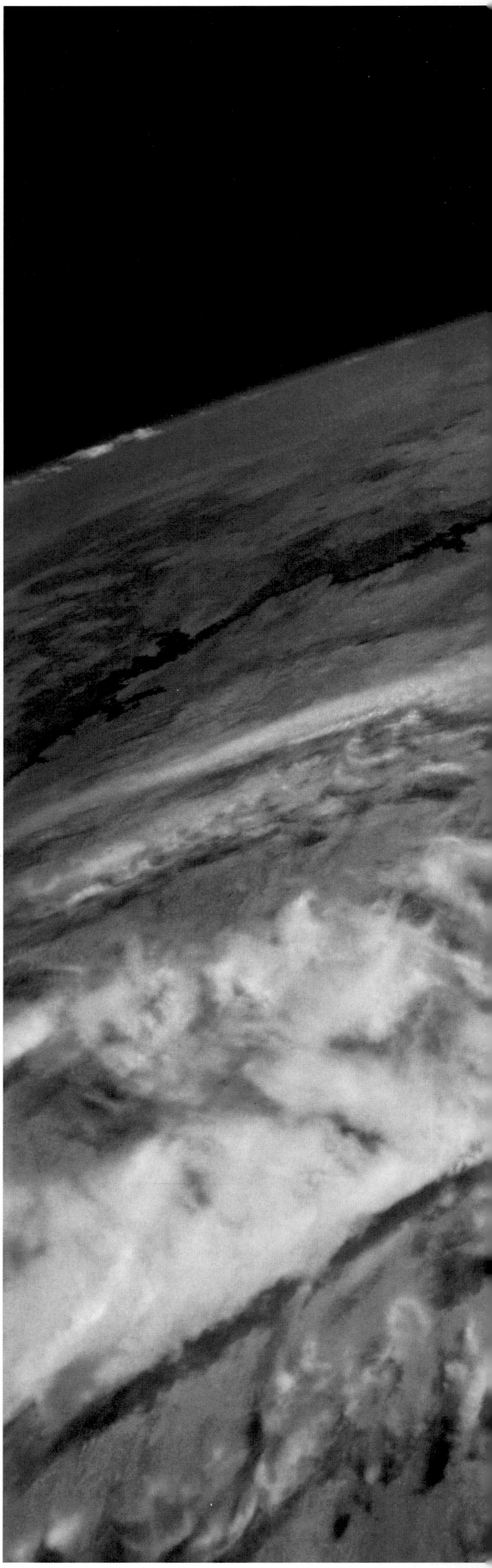

312 top The oasis of Bahariya is a little nucleus of green lost in the Western Desert of Egypt, where the sands extend for hundreds of kilometers.

312 bottom To the south of Marsa Matruh, the oasis of Siwa appears out of the dunes and sands of the desert. A few clouds throw small shadows on the scant areas with vegetation.

312-313 In the desert, beneath the clouds, is the Western Desert oasis of Dakhla. In the distance (above left) is the course of the Nile.

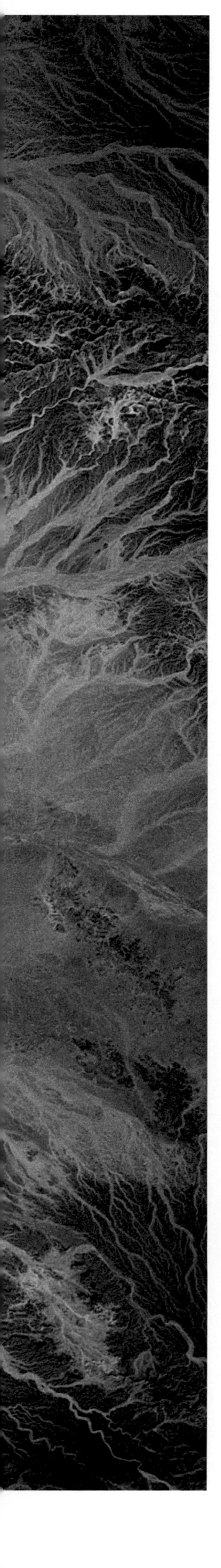

310 The bend in the Nile
at Qena, downstream
from Luxor (lower right),
occupies a broad sweep in
which the abundance of
water makes for lush
vegetation.

311 The Nile cuts into
the Eastern Desert of
Egypt with the bend of
Qena.

311

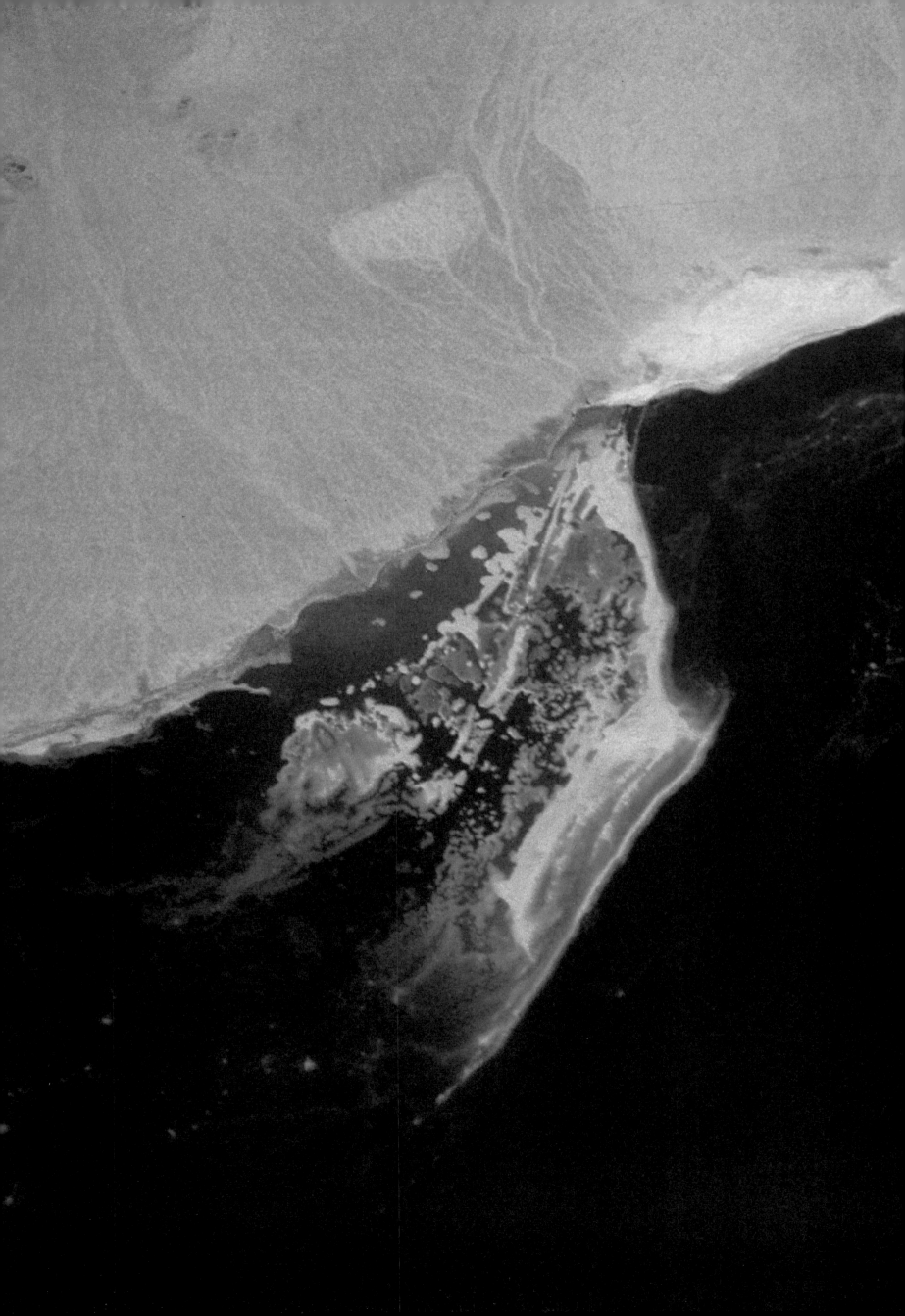

308 Viewed from the southwest, the peninsula of Ras Banas, which extends from the Egyptian coast into the Red Sea, interacts with currents and wave movement.

309 The coral barriers to the south of Ras Banas.

308

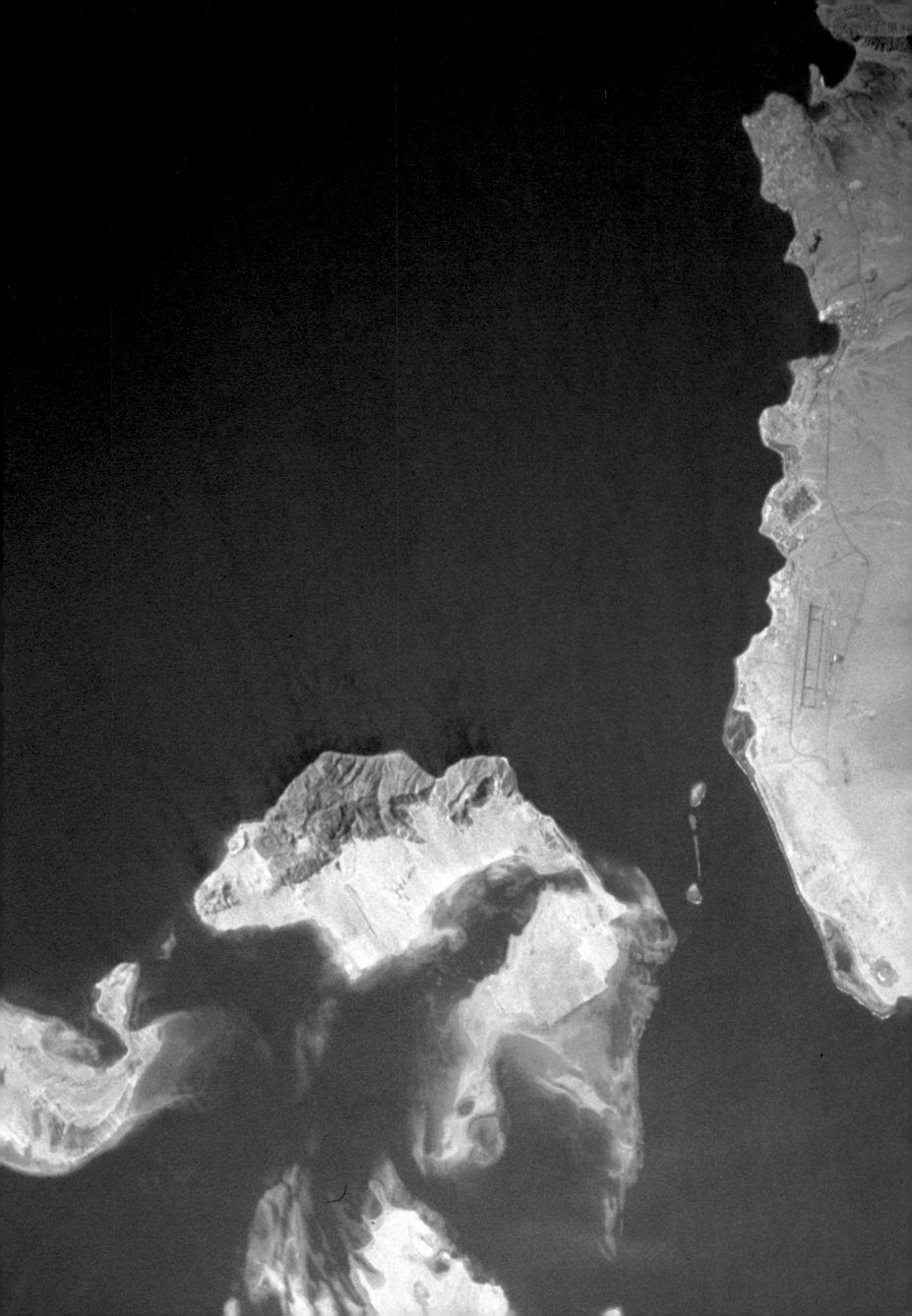

304-305 The Sinai Peninsula, made up of pre-Cambrian formations (gneiss, crystalline schist, with traces of granite and red amphibolic granite, diorite, and syenite), underwent intense movement and dense fractures in the Cenozoic era, which gave the reliefs and summits of the southern part of the peninsula a distinct shape. The highest summits reach 2,637 meters in Jebel Katherina and descend rocky, impervious, and arid toward the banks of the Gulf of Aqaba. The waters of the Red Sea seem intensely blue and the rocks and sands of Ras Muhammad stand out clearly.

305 Desert islands, sandbars, and shallow sea beds crowd the entrance to the Straits of Gubal, leading to the Gulf of Suez. The coast of Sinai appears at the top of the picture.

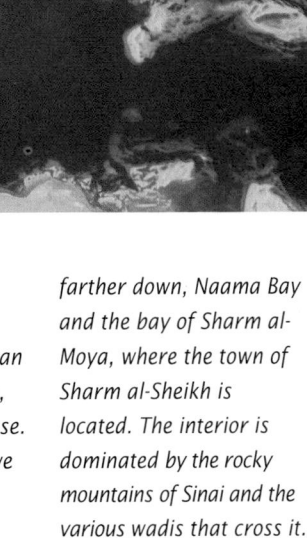

306-307 The Straits of Tiran, with the island of the same name, are the access to the Gulf of Aqaba (top center), which lies along the eastern coast of Sinai. To the right are the islands of Tiran and Sanafir and, between Sinai and Tiran, the Tiran reefs: Gordon, Jackson, Thomas, and Woodhouse. On the coast of Sinai we can see the airport of Sharm al-Sheikh and farther down, Naama Bay and the bay of Sharm al-Moya, where the town of Sharm al-Sheikh is located. The interior is dominated by the rocky mountains of Sinai and the various wadis that cross it.

232 A strip of cultivated land at the eastern end of Fayoum blends into the waters of Lake Qarun. The neat contrast with the tongues of dazzling sand forms the background.

232-233 The extensive oasis of Fayoum, which lies a hundred kilometers southeast of Cairo, is one of the most fertile regions in Egypt. About one-fifth is covered by Lake Qarun. The plots of cultivated land in the south of the oasis claim every possible square meter from the sand before suddenly giving way to the desert.

234 In its continual struggle with the desert, Lake Qarun is slowly shrinking. The gradual lowering of the water level can be clearly seen at the western tip.

235 top The surface of Lake Qarun lies forty-five meters below sea level; it separates the fertile zone from the desert, but its high salinity makes it useless for irrigation.

235 bottom A spate of green fields surrounds the largest town in the oasis, Medinet al-Fayoum. The town is crossed by the Bahr Yussuf, a distributary of the Nile.

236 In the desert to the southeast of Medinet al-Fayoum are several Coptic monasteries, including the monastery of the Archangel Gabriel seen here.

236-237 The large monastery of St. Samuel stands in the sands to the south of Fayoum.

238 Ruins of the temple dedicated to the cobra-goddess Renenutet and the croccdile-god Sobek in Medinet Madi, the town of Narmuthis in Greek papyruses. The temple was built by Amenemhat III and IV and enlarged during the Ptolemaic period.

239 top The temple complex stands on the desert plateau southwest of the oasis of Fayoum. The nucleus was built during the Middle Kingdom and the side buildings during the Ptolemaic and Roman ages.

239 bottom A series of sphinxes with human and lion heads lines the avenue to the temple and continues inside the courtyard as far as the monumental portal.

240 top View of the ancient Ptolemaic town of Tebtynis, with the temple in the background. Many papyruses in Demotic and ancient Greek have been found here.

240 bottom A pair of lion-headed sphinxes in front of the Tebtynis temple.

241 Ruins of the temple of Tebtynis, the town now called Tell Umm al-Burigat.

242-243 A large lake to the north of Lake Qarun, near Medinet Dimai, colored by mineral substances.

Sinai and the Red Sea

"And Moses stretched his hand over the sea; and the Lord caused the sea to go back . . . and the children of Israel went into the midst of the sea upon the dry ground: and the waters were a wall unto them on their right hand, and on their left . . . .And the waters returned, and covered the chariots, and the horsemen, and all the host of Pharaoh that came into the sea after them" (Exodus, 14, 21–28).

And thus, we learn, the Israelites reached Sinai in their flight to the Promised Land. Wedged between Asia and Africa, washed to the north by the Mediterranean and to the south by the Red Sea, the Sinai peninsula is a crossroads that has been the scene not only of biblical events but of comings and goings of all kinds throughout history.

The interior of Sinai is a combination of jagged mountain peaks, deserts of dunes and stone, and ancient fossil beaches where bushes and clusters of palms sometimes grow. Sedimentary limestone and sandstone alternate with volcanic granite and basalt in a medley of earthen and fiery colors. In this harsh but powerful landscape, many believe that the Lord appeared to Moses in the form of a burning bush and later gave him the Ten Commandments. But where and when these miraculous events took place is still debated.

The route of the Exodus is not clear. The Scriptures are contradictory and, naturally, no mention was made in Egyptian accounts of an event that was irrelevant to the children of Amun-Ra. This crucial event may have taken place during the reign of Ramesses II or his successor, Merenptah (Nineteenth Dynasty), but it must have occurred before 1250 BCE, when Jericho fell, as by then Moses had already died. The miraculous crossing of the *yam suf* ("sea of reeds") probably took place to the north of the Red Sea, somewhere around the Bitter Lakes or perhaps even on the Mediterranean coast near Lake Bardawil. From here the Israelites entered Sinai on a route that is debated according to how the sources are interpreted.

In the south of the peninsula, in the heart of the great circle of mountains that culminates in Jebel Katherina (Mount St. Catherine), stands the mountain now identified as the biblical Mount Sinai on which Moses received the Ten Commandments. Atop sheer granite walls at the summit of the mountain, stands a chapel dedicated to the Holy Trinity. It shares the superb panorama with the remains of a small mosque built, it is believed, over the cave in which Moses took refuge for forty days. Farther down, a small, verdant plateau surrounded by rough rock spires is the site of St. Stephen's retreat, shaded by cypress and olive trees.

At the foot of the mountain stands St. Catherine's monastery, the holiest place in Sinai, built on the supposed site of the burning bush. The order of Greek Orthodox monks who still live in the monastery was founded by the early Christian empress Helena in 330 but it was the Byzantine emperor Justinian who, three centuries later, transformed the retreat into a fortified complex. The various buildings of the monastery and the basilica lie within a high wall protected by battlements and either intersect with one another or are separated by a maze of corridors, courtyards, trees, and flowers. In front of the church, an eleventh-century mosque represents the third religion of the site, Islam, which recognizes Moses and Jesus as being sent as prophets by God before Muhammad. The library in the monastery includes a valuable collection of manuscripts second only to that in the Vatican.

The remains of St. Catherine, martyred in Alexandria, lie in the church after angels, as tradition has it, transported her body to the top of Mount St. Catherine, the highest peak in Egypt, where the monks found it. They brought it down to the basilica and enclosed it in a chest that lies in the choir. During the age of the Crusades, the cult of St. Catherine spread to Europe and, with Rome and Jerusalem, the monastery became one of the most famous places of pilgrimage in Christendom.

In addition to its religious resonances, the wild land of Sinai bears traces of an eventful past. Its geographical position has always made it a natural frontier between Egypt and the Middle East, besides being a place of transit, refuge, and dispute.

The recent history of the Suez Canal and the Sinai peninsula is marked by the long conflict between Egypt and Israel. This was concluded in 1978 with the peace treaty signed at Camp David under the aegis of the United Nations. Even today, an international and independent organization named the Multinational Force & Observers is stationed in the Sinai to ensure respect for the treaty and, in particular, unimpeded maritime access at the entrance to the Gulf of Aqaba.

The routes taken by modern military forces are the same as those used by armies in the ancient world. South of the great lagoon area of Lake Bardawil on the Mediterranean coast, there lie the ruins of the forts that protected "Path of Horus," one of the ancient military and commercial routes that connected the Nile Valley with Asia Minor. Egyptians, Persians, Greeks, Arabs, and many more of the great movements that marked the history of the Mediterranean basin passed this way.

Farther south, the deep ravines of the western valleys between Wadi Nasb and Wadi Maghara hide the immense

244 Yolanda Reef and Shark Reef off the extreme southerly point of Sinai are between 20-30 meters in depth. The strong currents and presence of sharks make diving in this area a demanding activity.

deposits of turquoise, copper, and malachite that attracted rulers to these desolate areas from earliest antiquity. The region was never truly colonized by the Egyptians but there are many traces of their exploitation of the area's mineral wealth, particularly in the area of Serabit al-Khadim, where the ruins of the famous "Lady of Turquoise" temple dedicated to Hathor lie. Nearby there are the remains of the quarries, foundries, and the small village where the workers lived. A large number of graffiti and rock inscriptions cover the walls of the surrounding canyons, recording a history of mining in the area from the Third Dynasty with few interruptions until the end of the New Kingdom.

The most extraordinary aspect of Sinai is that its archaeological heritage, rich with biblical and historical references (though modest when compared to the great monuments of the Nile Valley), is enhanced by its majestic setting. An example is the splendid canyon of Wadi Feran that connects the Gulf of Suez to St. Catherine's monastery. This is the largest ravine in the peninsula and twists between the rocky mountains dominated by Jebel Serbal. At the foot of the massif, the route is sprinkled with ruins, churches, the tombs of Christians and Muslims, and small monasteries in the branches of a lush oasis. Dense copses of palms and tamarind trees provide shade for the simple huts in which one of the many tribes of Bedouin that inhabit the Sinai region live.

The eastern side of the peninsula contains other surprises, such as the Colored Canyon, which is a long valley cut through the layers of sandstone by the passage of water. The rock walls, painted in warm tones by nature, widen and contract until at their narrowest point they are no more than a meter apart. Flying over the rocky pinnacles of the area to the east of St. Catherine's, one's gaze is attracted by great patches of an unusual color—sky blue—in the ocher desert. This is the Blue Valley, in which lumps of rock were painted the color of peace by a Belgian artist in 1980 to celebrate the end of the war between Egypt and Israel.

The fantastic world of sand and rock that dominates Sinai is fringed by white beaches and sheer cliffs that form the boundary of an underwater paradise. This is Sinai's other natural treasure and its major tourist attraction.

The warm, clear waters of the Red Sea separate the African coast from the Arabian peninsula for 2,500 kilometers. They split at the southern tip of Sinai into the two gulfs of Aqaba and Suez to form a marine environment based on formations of a stony coral and populated by thousands of species of fish. The formation of this long, narrow sea passage is the result of the slow drift of the Arabian plate away from the continental African platform, thus creating a deep fracture filled by the waters of the Red Sea. The Red Sea opens into the Indian Ocean through the Bab al-Mandeb Straits but it is considered a closed sea, and, though belonging biologically to the Indo-Pacific region, its fauna is roughly 20 percent endemic.

The balances of marine life in the Gulf of Suez have been compromised by the sea traffic that continually passes through the Suez Canal, but the shores of the Gulf of Aqaba (which reaches 1800 meters in depth) offer marvellous marine landscapes of coral reefs and tropical fish in an explosion of life and color that transforms the depths into dazzling underwater gardens.

To defend these paradises from the risks associated with tourism in the area, the Ras Muhammad National Park has been created to safeguard the area at the southern tip of Sinai where the delicate balances between the marine and terrestrial ecosystems are strictly protected by law. The promontory of Ras Muhammad is what remains of a coral reef that emerged from the great Tethys Sea around seventy million years ago and its rocks still contain many shells and fossilised species of coral. The bays and deep inlets along the jagged coastline provide views of changing colors, green oases of mangroves, turquoise lagoons, intense aquamarine depths, and coral beds that break-up the surface of the water into all hues of blue.

The sea depths feature large reefs of stony coral either in terraces not far beneath the surface or on steeply rising scarps at depths of up to 100 meters. Swimming among the pink, red, and gold corals, anemones, and sea-fans, the tropical fauna is dominated by the brilliantly colored carousels of jack fish, parrot fish, and angel fish, and the austere shapes of Napoleon fish and irascible morays; it is, however, becoming increasingly rare to see the grey sharks that at one time inhabited the reefs at the southern tip of Sinai.

The most interesting area for diving enthusiasts lies a few kilometers east of the park at Sharm al-Sheikh, at one time a small fishing village. In just a few years it has stretched along the coast as far as Naama Bay and Sheikh Coast to form an unbroken string of hotels, tourist villages, and shopping centers. Yet even if it is being affected by the mass influx of tourists, the long ribbon of beaches, low cliffs, and small bays as far as the cape of Ras Nasrani is the entry to an underwater universe of coral reefs and wide passageways. Here luxuriant colonies of multicolored alcyonaria, sea whips, and gorgonias are populated by marine "chameleons," butterfly fish, long nose hawkfish, and the elongated profile of the trumpet fish.

The island of Tiran lies opposite Ras Nasrani; it is

formed by four coral reefs that are the jewel of the region for their abundance of color and marine life. The strong currents make diving difficult but form the most favorable environmental conditions if one is to see examples of deep sea fish. The two outer reefs are littered with the wrecks of ships that have foundered on the northern side.

Flying north up the coast, one comes to Dahab, where tourism is beginning to take hold in three Bedouin oases of straw-roofed stone buildings.

The site is surrounded by high mountains and desert landscapes such as Wadi Nasb. This is the widest point on the gulf (28 kilometers) and the coastline of gentle beaches and coral falls within the protected area of Ras Abu Galum. One of the more interesting excursions for divers is the Canyon, a crack in the rock up to 50 meters in depth, biologically rich in large multicolored dermosponges.

On a level with the Blue Valley, the two residential centers of Nuweiba al-Tarabin—overlooked by a solid Arab-Ottoman fort—and Nuweiba al-Muzeini are separated by a broad desert zone where it is not unusual to see herds of camels.

The magnificent landscapes of the interior are a fascinating alternative to the underwater environment, offering the opportunity to explore oases or to understand the customs of the Bedouin who live among the sands and mountains.

Bedouin communities are especially numerous in the last stretch of Egypt before the border with Israel, where the coast is a succession of bays and open areas of alluvial origin. Taba, on the border, is the largest tourist center. Its main attraction is Pharaoh's Island, where the ruins of an ancient Crusader castle stand above the magnificent coral reefs of the island.

On the African coast of the Red Sea, the strong currents and reefs have caused numberless wrecks over the centuries, many of which can still be seen at just a few meters' depth. Many can be explored from the Straits of Gubal at the mouth of the Gulf of Suez down to north of Hurghada in an exciting archaeological adventure for more expert divers. The skeletons of the ships from all ages blend with the black coral and colorful alcyonaria that grow profusely in this area where the current is strong, offering refuge to a great variety of sea creatures, including dolphins and sea turtles.

Hurghada, settled in Ptolemaic times, lies 600 kilometers from Cairo and over the last few years has experienced massive tourist development. The interior is still wild, with high mountains where the Romans came to quarry the white and purple flecked porphyry loved by the emperors. Kilometers of transparent lagoons soften the dark blue of the sea, where steep underwater walls are lined with multicolor corals.

Farther to the south is the wide bay of Qusayr, where pilgrims to Mecca embarked to cross the Red Sea during the Middle Ages. The seabed here is sandy, though dotted with surprising reefs that stretch out towards Safaga in lush colonies of black coral.

At the southern tip of the Egyptian Red Sea, the reefs nearest the coast are less varied compared to those in the north but, away from the shore or around the islands, the seabed is formed by enormous terraces of moonlike coral. This is a paradise for colorful tropical fish, jack fish, turtles, barracuda (for which it is an ideal habitat), and various species of deep-sea fish including the fearsome hammerhead shark.

One of the pearls of this area close to the Sudanese border is the island of Zebirget, the famous Topazos of Pliny the Elder, where the mysterious "emeralds of the evening" were mined. "Emeralds of the evening" are olivine gems with a greenish-yellow glow that shine in the dark. Sought by the pharaohs and the Romans and brought to Europe by Crusaders, olivines were charged with religious and miraculous powers that made them the symbol of St. Matthew and, in heraldry, the stone of faith and magnanimity.

The arid and lunar appearance of the island, and the presence of a mineral typical of the depths of the earth's crust—peridotite—suggest that it was pushed up from the depths by the movement of the continental plates. In 1998 the island was made a marine park, and now it is inhabited exclusively by large colonies of terns, seagulls, ospreys, and, during summer nights, by turtles, which come here to lay their eggs. Under the water are incredible spires and domes of coral; this is the haunt of tropical grouper fish, octopuses, and many varieties of echinoderms and molluscs.

As in many other areas of the Red Sea, the protection of the island is the result of a policy of environmental conservation that is indispensable to the preservation of the sea's extraordinary and unique biological wealth.

Thanks to their ability to regenerate themselves, coral reefs form one of the most stable ecosystems in nature, but the delicate balance between corals and reef inhabitants make them also one of the most fragile. That is why, in addition to the stringent restrictions imposed by the government, tourists should feel responsible for and respectful of the environment they are visiting, which, it is hoped, future generations will still be able to enjoy.

248-249 Water, sky, and land merge in a profusion of blue on the Red Sea coast at Ras Gharib, north of Hurghada.

*250 The coast in front of
Ras Gemsa promontory in
the Gubal Strait.
The coral barrier is
broken up by islands and
channels.*

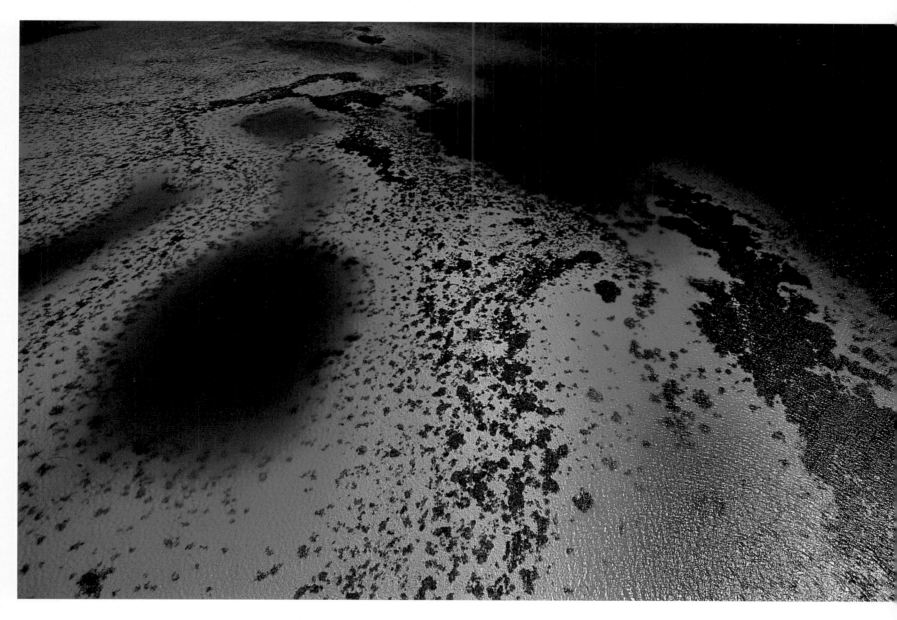

251 The coral reef to
the north of Hurghada.
The coral formations on
the sea bed create
elaborate geometric
patterns in continual
change.

252-253 The changing
coral universe in the
Gubal Strait. The barrier
is formed by a series of
reefs whose nature is
determined by the
characteristics of the sea
floor, the light, and the
water temperature.

254-255 A long line of hotels and tourist complexes has drastically altered the coastline of the Red Sea from Hurghada to al-Gouna twenty kilometers north. The sea and its bed are still beautiful, but life has suffered in the sections where divers are most congested.

255 top The lighthouse on the island of Ashrafi opposite the point of Ras Gemsa barely rises above the water where the Gulf of Suez enters the Red Sea.

255 bottom Steep underwater walls lined with alcyonaria and gorgonia and broad stretches of sandbank are typical of the much visited Giftun Island off Hurghada.

256 The stranded hull of the Hedoromo Million Hope is all that remains of one of the ships that have run aground on the coral banks along the coastline of Naqb.

257 top The mangrove forest that grows in the area of Naqb, north of Naama Bay. In order to protect the delicate environmental balance, this stretch of the coast has been made a National Park.

257 center These mangroves have the capacity to absorb seawater and expel the salt through their leaves. By holding the sediment in place with their roots, they are an effective barrier against erosion.

257 bottom The oases and lagoons of Naqb National Park teem with life; the large variety of birds includes herons, storks, and ospreys.

258-259 Alternative Reef, on the west coast of the Ras Muhammad promontory in Sinai. This area is characterized by extensive coral banks and a rich variety of reef life.

260 A section of the east coast of Ras Muhammad near Ras Atar. The coral barrier drops nearly 45 meters and is home to many colonies of gorgonia.

261 top Mangrove Island is separated from the promontory by a channel. Its many mangroves filter the seawater and expel the salt crystals through their leaves.

261 bottom Ras Muhammad Park extends into the Red Sea between the Gulf of Suez and the Gulf of Aqaba. Its seabed has an extraordinary variety of corals and deep sea and reef fauna.

262-263 Ras Muhammad promontory is formed by a fossil coral reef 50 meters high. On the tip is the Shark Observatory, and to the left Main Beach.

264-265 Anemone City, between Shark Reef and the outlet of Hidden Bay, is a coral bank with a dense population of anemones.

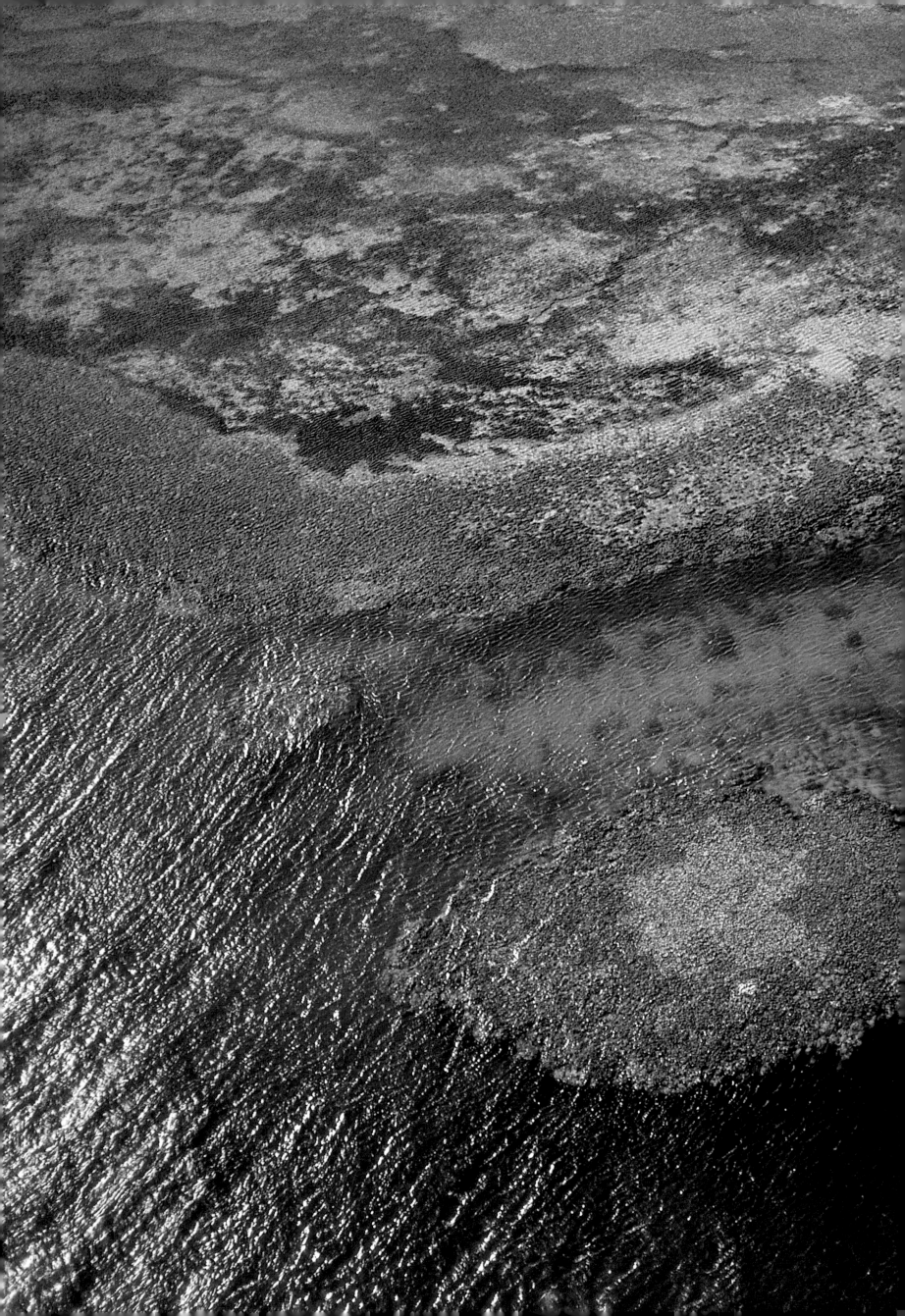

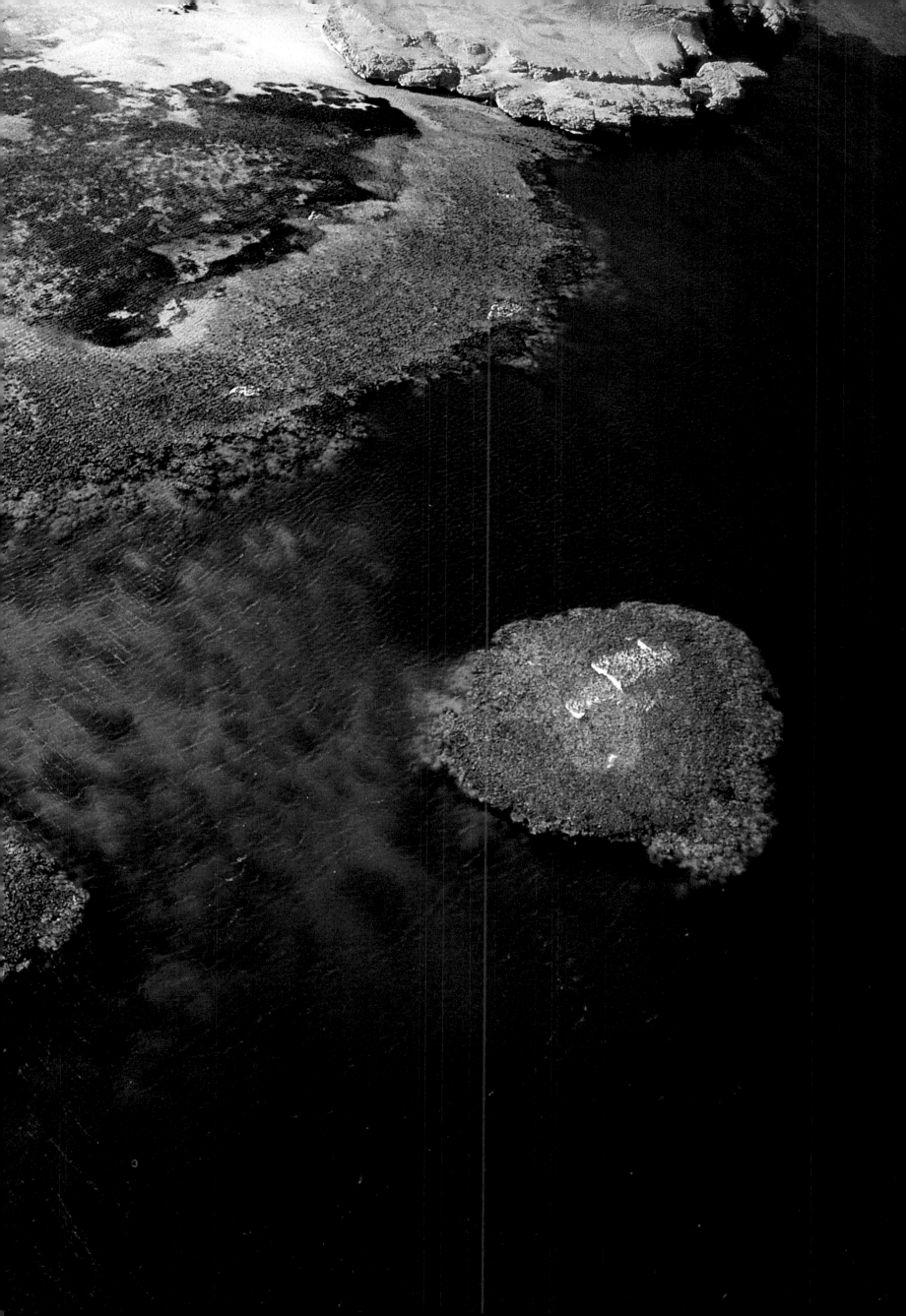

266 top A carpet of houses and hotels covers the east cliff of Sharm al-Moya. In the background, the lighthouse of Ras Umm Sidd. The promontory has an extensive coral barrier, in particular on the coast to the west of the lighthouse.

266 bottom Sharm al-Sheikh bay, with a military port where the Egyptian coastguard and multinational forces are permanently based.

266-267 The first nucleus of what was to become the largest tourist area in Sinai—

Sharm al-Sheikh—was built in the bay of Sharm al-Moya.

268-269 The wide Naama Bay lies few kilometers to the north of Sharm. In just a few years the city has become the largest tourist center in southern Sinai.

270-271 *The coastline from Sharm al-Sheikh to Naama Bay has been colonized by large hotel chains that compete in fantastic architectural designs and offer sea lovers all kinds of facilities. On the right you can admire the Jolie Ville Mövenpick Golf Hotel & Resort.*

272-273 bottom The wonderful Gordon Reef; this is the southernmost of the four coral banks in the Tiran Strait between the island of the same name and the cape of Ras Nasrani. A wreck lies on its north edge.

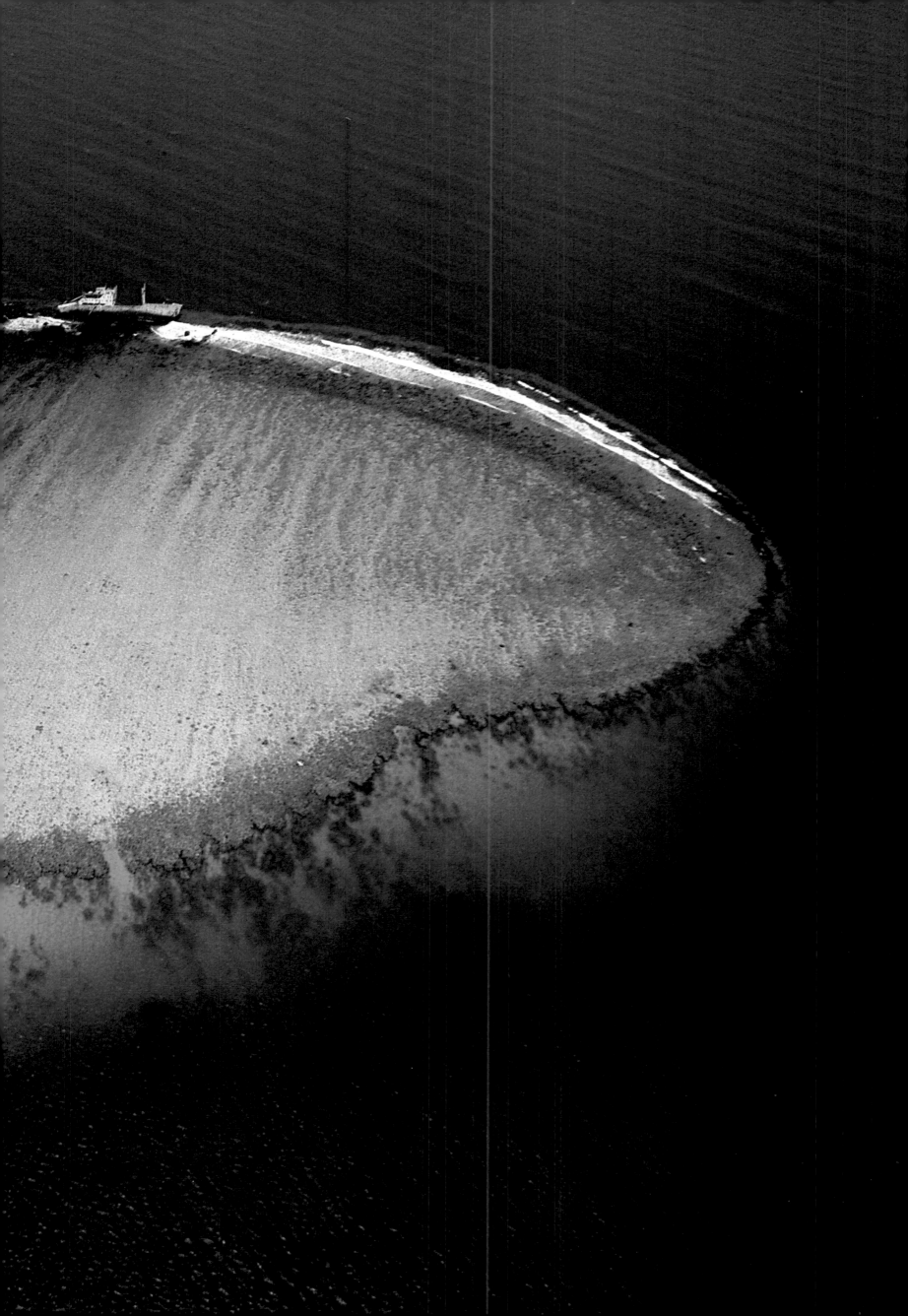

274-275 and 275 top
Tiran Island, with the
smaller Sanafir Island, at
the mouth of the Gulf of
Aqaba between the
coasts of Sinai and Saudi
Arabia (to which it legally
belongs).

275 bottom A fossil coral
platform and deep inlets
are typical of the coast of
Tiran Island; the island is
an untouched and
vigorous biological oasis
thanks to its protected
ecosystem.

276-277 Tiran Island.
Its strategic position
in the center of
the strait means
it is closely guarded
militarily.

278 top The Bedouin village of Assalah looks onto the bay of Ghazala north of Dahab. Recently developed, tourism has not overwhelmed Dahab and offers several alternatives to resort life.

278 bottom Hotels and resorts at Dahab. The tourist facilities are more modest on the whole than in other destinations on the Red Sea, yet they offer excellent opportunities for diving.

278-279 The superb al-Qura Bay at Dahab is popular with windsurfers. The richness and variety of the reef life offer divers splendid outings.

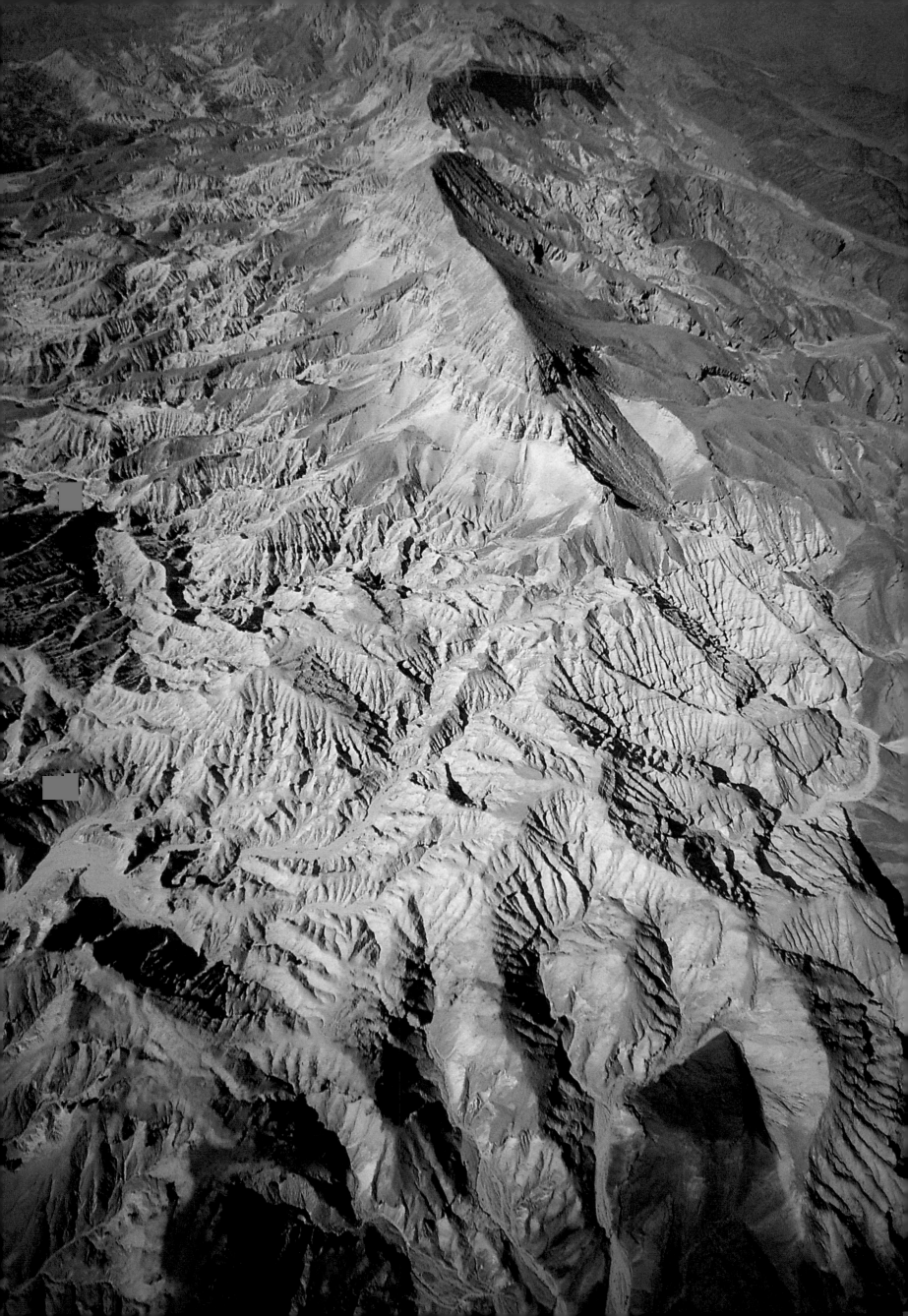

280 Rocky mountain crests of southwest Sinai near al-Tor. Numerous wadis in the mountains run straight into the Gulf of Suez.

281 The floor of Wadi Feiran is an oasis of palms, the largest in Sinai. It was a stop on the journey of pilgrims heading toward St. Catherine's monastery.

282-283 The desert in the area of al-Tor at the tip of Sinai is made up of Quaternary formations of ancient coral sediments.

284-285 St. Catherine's monastery was founded at the foot of Jebel Musa (Mount Moses), where it is believed God revealed himself to Moses in the form of the Burning Bush.

286-287 The weak light of dawn softens the spectacular mountains in the center of Sinai.

Egypt from Space

text by Giulio Melegari Mazzoni
photo by Nasa

The earliest cartographic documents to have survived to the modern day, in the form of rudimentary and approximate maps, were made by the Egyptians. It was in the areas seen in the following satellite photographs that the first human skills were developed relating to the surveying, recording, and symbolic reproduction of the dimensional and morphological features of the land and sea with the aim of allowing sailors and travelers to follow routes that had already been explored. Long before photography was invented, cartography had become an exact and objective science used for the various military, political, economic, and scientific purposes, for which geographical, chorographic, and topographic maps were produced.

A cartographic document is—by definition and in concept—a flat representation that is reduced, approximate, and symbolic of a section of the earth's surface, produced using various types of geometric projection to highlight particular aspects (consequently to the detriment of others) and inevitably entailing a two-dimensional approximation of three-dimensional features on a convex surface. From the early surveying techniques using traditional methods of topography and trigonometric measurements, further developments have led to aerial photogrammetry, and more recently, to GIS (Geographical Information System) methods based on satellite photography.

Traditional topography and cartography are typically a synthesis of a body of information and measurements that condenses all the information relevant to the user into a graphic document. Users can then base their analysis, research, or practical application on this graphic summary document. Photographs taken from a great height allow the concepts of synthesis and analysis to coexist in a reduced representation of reality, but the image is no longer flat, approximate, or symbolic. Depending on the purposes for which the satellite photographs are to be used, their resolution will vary, they will have different possibilities for enlargement, be taken at particular angles, and will allow certain chromatic, morphological, or other features to be emphasized or attenuated. The intuitive and perceptive immediacy of a satellite photograph—which reveals in an undistorted image an area so great that it would require many weeks to cross it on foot—gives an instantaneous summary of features that would require intense and prolonged calculation for them to be deduced from geographical, physical, political, historical, or geological maps.

Egypt, including Sinai, and its contiguous areas of the Arabian Peninsula, the Red Sea, and the Gulf of Aden have been the theater of continuous events in the history of humanity, and before that, in the history of the physical world in which we live. The separation of Arabia from Africa and the opening of the Red Sea and Gulf of Aden in the late Cenozoic era were accompanied by earth movements along the Red Sea fault line, resulting in extreme dislocations and rifts whose geometric development is immediately evident in the chromatic contrast between the arms of the sea, the physical geography of the mountains, and the desert areas.

A similar chromatic contrast reveals the environment in which the three-thousand year kingdom based in the Nile Valley flourished.

The Delta stands out in the shape of a gigantic fan, approximately 250 kilometers in length along the coast and 160 kilometers in depth from north to south; it lies at the end of a river course that winds and bends through yellow desert and brown rocky mountain chains that still bear the signs of dendritic surface water channels from the past.

No cartographic representation can equal the effect of an image that shows continental and peninsular Egypt in the context of the eastern Mediterranean, complete with the effect created by the curvature of the Earth and the realistic view of the surface contours. We see the Eastern Desert, the Western Desert and its oases, the course of the Nile, the Delta, and the Suez Canal. Coupling these environmental images with the area's social and anthropological history, close attention to particular areas will form the basis for an analysis of features and facts of specific interest connected to the area's geography, urbanization, hydrography, structural geology, and geomorphology.

288 In an impressive panorama, we look south along the Red Sea, bordered on the east (to the left) by the huge stretch of the Arabian Peninsula. To the right is the Nile; to the left of the river is the Eastern Desert.

290-291 The line of the Suez Canal is unmistakable in this view looking south to the southern Mediterranean shore.
Near the mouth of the Suez Canal is Port Said, and to the right is the Nile Delta.

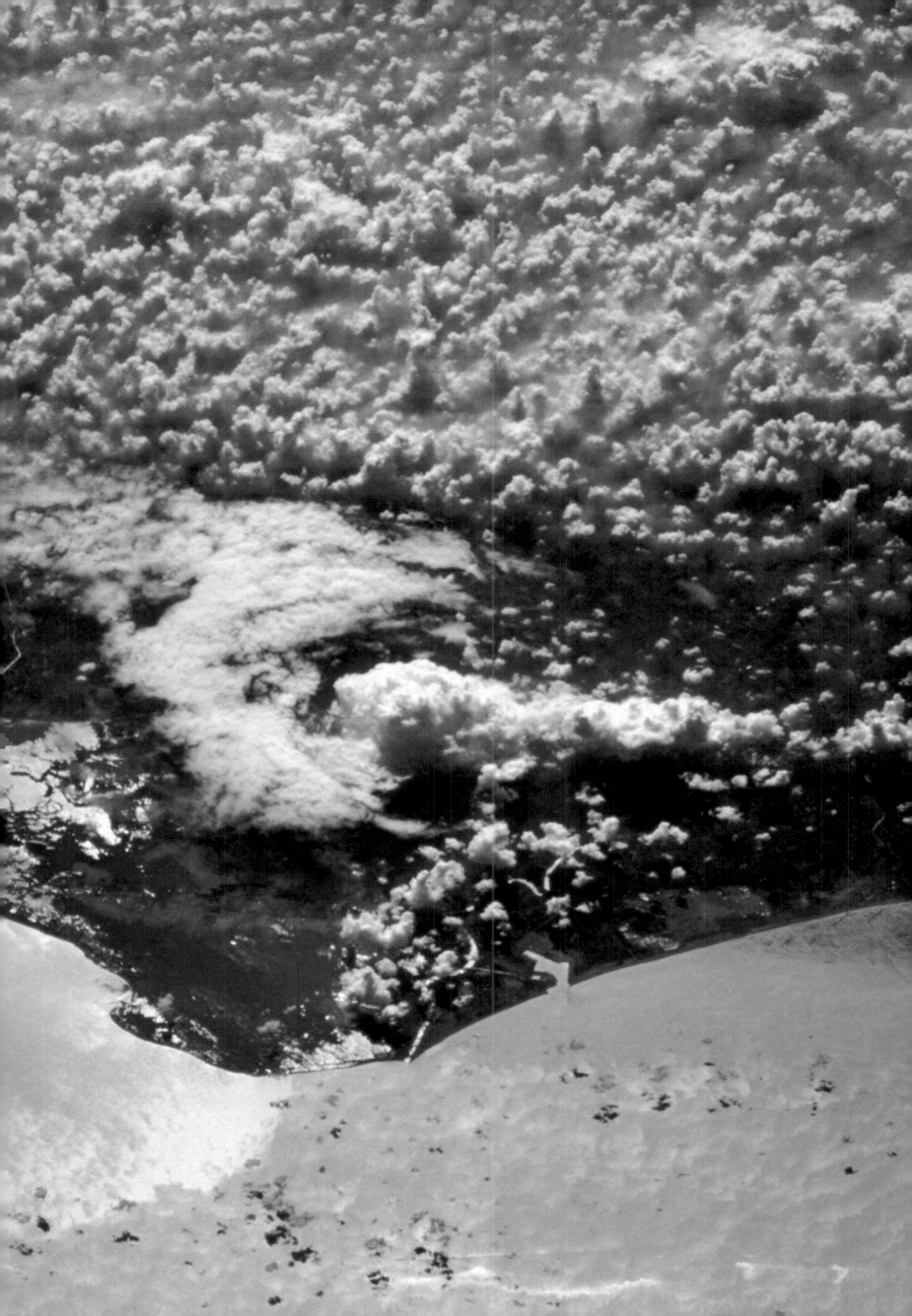

292 top Looking southeast, the satellite camera takes in the Sinai Peninsula and the northern extremes of the Red Sea.

292 bottom The Nile Delta stands out against the sands of northern Egypt. The coast of Turkey and the island of Cyprus are clearly visible near the top of the picture.

292-293 This impressive view from the space shuttle shows almost all of Egypt, including the Western and Eastern Deserts, the Nile Valley and the Fayoum basin, Sinai, the Gulfs of Suez and Aqaba, and the Red Sea.

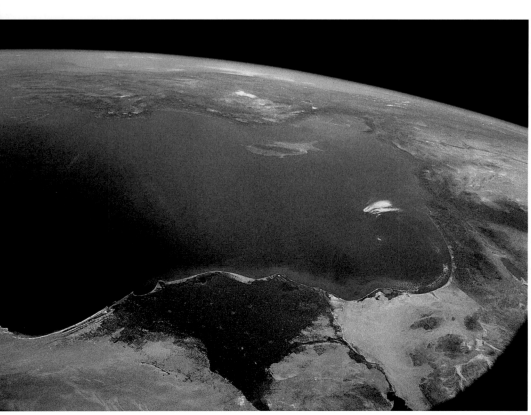

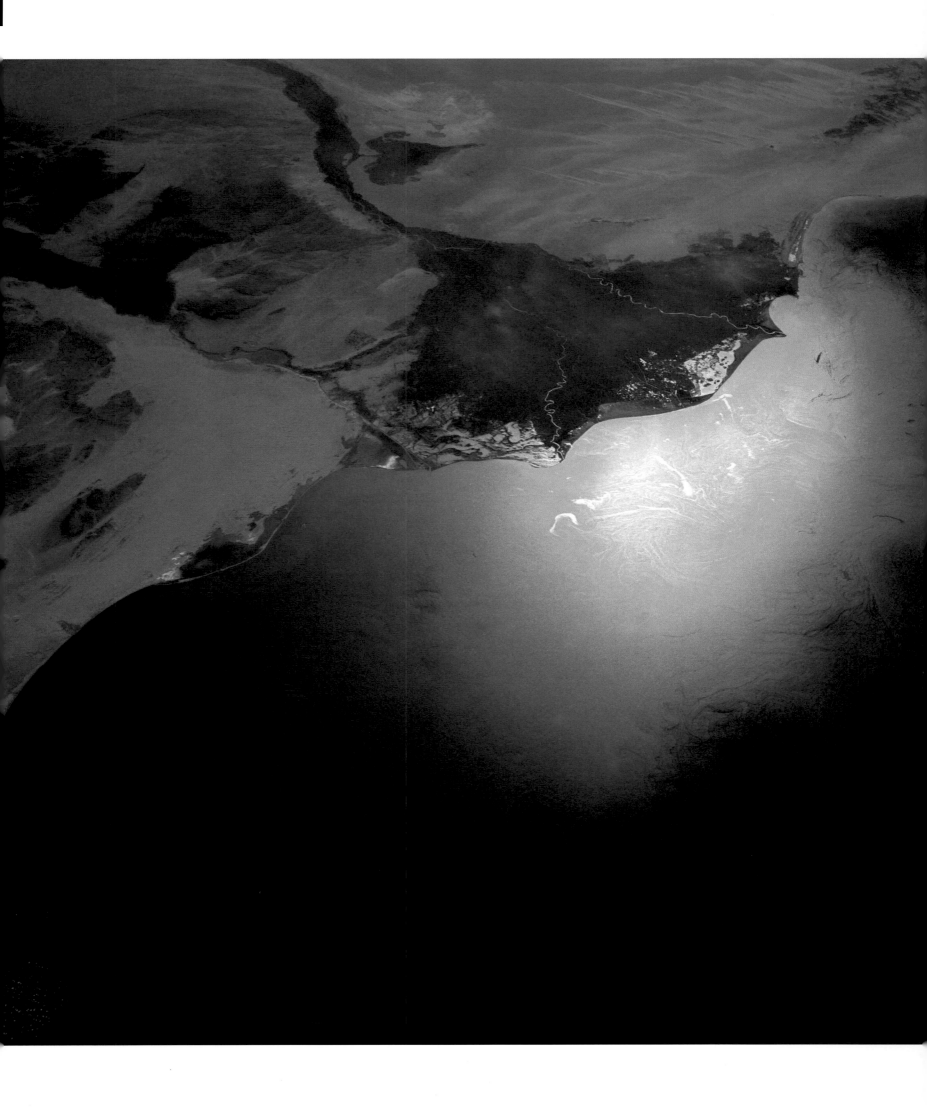

294-295 *The northern part of Sinai, the Suez Canal, and the Nile Delta from the northeast. The two main branches of the Nile (Damietta, left, and Rashid, right) are clearly discernible.*

295 *The play of light and shallow water show up sandbanks and traces on the seabed along the coast between Alexandria and Marsa Matruh.*

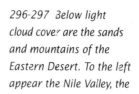

296-297 Below light
cloud cover are the sands
and mountains of the
Eastern Desert. To the left
appear the Nile Valley, the

Fayoum basin, and the
beginning of the Delta.
To the right is the Gulf of
Suez, with the entrance to
the Suez Canal at its head.

297 Looking northwest
along the Red Sea, we
can clearly see the
tectonic nature of the
clean cut between the
landmasses of Egypt to
the left and the Arabian

Peninsula to the right.
At the top right is the
Sinai Peninsula and
beyond it the Nile Valley
and Delta. Luxor lies on
the southern curve of the
great bend in the river.

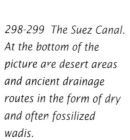

298-299 The Suez Canal. At the bottom of the picture are desert areas and ancient drainage routes in the form of dry and often fossilized wadis.

299 The northern coast of Sinai, where the peninsula slopes down from its arid rocky heights toward a plateau of sandy desert, followed by a strip of beach,

extending from Port Said in the west to Gaza in the east. Looking north, the picture shows the bars and lagoons of this low-lying coast.

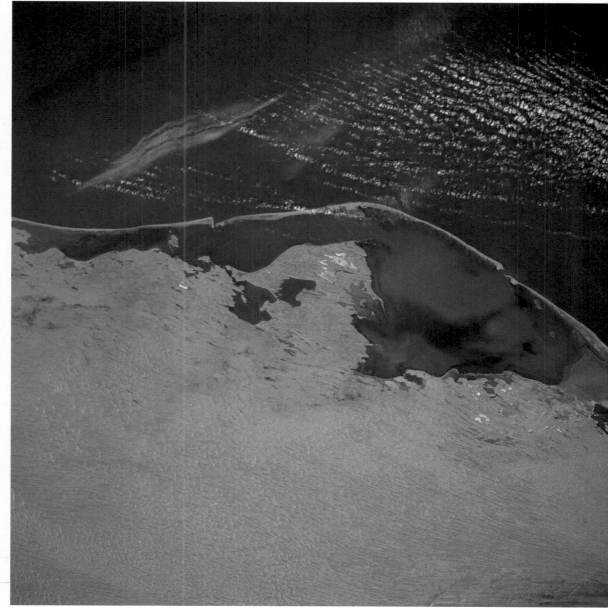

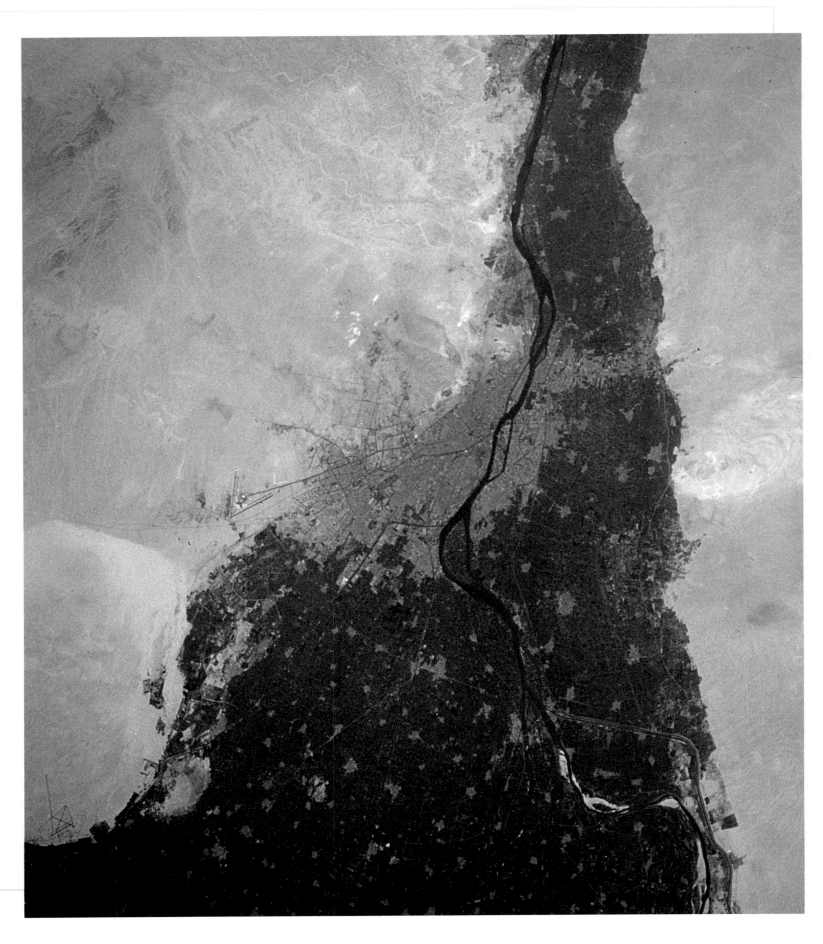

300 Greater Cairo
stretches out along
both banks of the Nile
as its Valley opens
out into the Delta.
The biggest city in Africa,
it has a population of
approximately 15 million
and occupies an area of
more than 200 square
kilometers.

301 Alexandria is located
at the western extremity
of the Nile Delta, on a strip
of shore that separates the
Mediterranean from the
Maryut Lagoon. In this
view looking north, deep
sea beds of the coast are
indicated by the
darkening shade of
the water.

302-303 This view north
shows the Sinai Peninsula
and the Gulfs of Aqaba
and Suez. We can see the
coral reefs and the islands
near Hurghada, the cape
of Ras Muhammad (the

extreme spur of Sinai),
and the islands of Tiran
and Sanafir at the mouth
of the Gulf of Aqaba.
The Nile, its Delta, and
the Fayoum basin are
visible to the left.